The
FIRE of
TRUTH

Sermons by Raymond Bryan Brown
Edited by Richard A. Spencer

BROADMAN PRESS
Nashville, Tennessee

Contents

Raymond Bryan Brown

A Curriculum Vitae

Dr. Brown was born in Winnfield, Louisiana, on November 16, 1923, and died on December 16, 1977, in Raleigh, North Carolina. He was educated at Louisiana State University (A.B., 1944), Yale Divinity School (B.D., 1947; S.T.M., 1948), The Southern Baptist Theological Seminary (Th.D., 1950), and engaged in postdoctoral study at the University of Tübingen. He married Caralie Nelson on September 2, 1946, and to them were born three children: Bonnie Nancye (Mrs. Stephen B. Gay, II), Raymond Bryan Brown, Jr. (deceased), and Helen Anne (Mrs. Richard Dale Kelly).

His pastoral ministry began at Beth Car Baptist Church in Halifax, Virginia (1950-52). From there he went to the University of Richmond to assume the position of assistant professor of Bible and religion (1952-55). During the years 1955-60, he served as pastor of Tabernacle Baptist Church in Richmond, Virginia. In 1960 he returned to the classroom, there to find his place of service until his death. At The Southern Baptist Theological Seminary in Louisville, Kentucky, he held the position of associate professor of New Testament interpretation (1960-64). In 1964 Professor Brown went to Southeastern Baptist Theological Seminary in Wake Forest, North Carolina, as professor of New Testament interpretation (1964-73) and later as distinguished professor of New Testament interpretation (1973-77). From 1966 until 1974 he served that school in the capacity of academic dean. A man of deep commitment to Christ and genuine love for Bible study, he was often invited to write for religious periodicals and was frequently enlisted as a Bible teacher and lecturer at religious assemblies, pastors' conferences, and on college and university campuses.

Professor Brown's scholastic abilities were widely recognized. He was honored by Phi Kappa Phi, Omicron Delta Kappa, and listed in *Contemporary Authors* (1968), the *Directory of American Scholars* (1974), *Outstanding Educators of America* (1974), and *Who's Who in Religion* (1977). His writings include *Professor in the Pulpit* (which he coedited with W. Morgan Patterson in 1963), *A Study of the New Testament* (which he coauthored with Velma Darbo in 1965), the commentary on 1 Corinthians in *The Broadman Bible Commentary* (1970), and *Mark: Savior for Sinners* (1978). He served as Bible editor of the *Encyclopedia of Southern Baptists* (Vol. III) and was a member of the Historical Commission from 1956 until 1960. Professional organizations of which he was a member include the Association of Baptist Professors of Religion (of which he was president in 1971) and the Society of Biblical Literature.

Introduction

This volume of sermons and addresses has been produced with a single purpose, to glorify God by extending the ministering labors of one of his trusted servants who has now "crossed the finish line of faith." The preaching, teaching, and writings of Raymond Bryan Brown touched the lives of many people. It is in appreciation for him and his work for our Lord, and in the hope that the extension of his labors may encourage even more men and women to faith and service for Christ that this collection is presented.

Dr. Brown was greatly appreciated by his students and parishioners for his faithfulness in the service of our Lord, whose cross and resurrection ever remained at the center of his proclamation. Ray taught with the heart of a pastor and preached with the keen mind of a scholar, using all the tools at his disposal to expound the Word of God. He exemplified the truth of what C. K. Barrett once said, that the true biblical scholar is a preacher or he has misunderstood his own subject, because the Bible demands to be preached; likewise, the biblical preacher who is worthy of his office is a scholar.[1]

Inspiration for this collection of sermons came from a growing awareness of the profound influence which Dr. Brown's teaching and preaching have had on the many lives he touched. His strong emphasis on the spiritual and intellectual preparation of God's servants and his energetic, thoughtful teaching of the Scriptures left many lasting impressions. These sermons have meant so very much to those who were present at the time of their presentation that they merit wider circulation. Some Christians as far away as Japan readily recall ideas and even phrases from these sermons which were preached many years earlier. I recall quite vividly that at the time of my mother's death a comforting note from my brother in Christ Dr. Alton Hood, a medical missionary in Thailand, included a quotation which he remembered Ray Brown using many years before, a quotation which derives from "A Little Child Shall Lead Them," Ray's funeral sermon for his infant son in 1957.

Most of these sermons (chapters 4 through 20) are transcriptions of seminary chapel sermons delivered at Southeastern Baptist Theological Seminary during the years 1965-1976. They are excellent examples of Brown's attempt to bring together austere and responsible thinking about our faith (stewardship of the mind) and Christian worship and service (stewardship of the heart). In his preaching, he did not aim to transform the sanctuary into a lecture hall but to proclaim the gospel in such a way that he would deliver meaningfully to God's people the benefits, insights, and discoveries of theological study. It was his calling, as he saw it, to bring the blessings of lofty, divine thoughts to bear significantly on everyday living.

Dr. Brown was a man of great vitality, energy, and wit. These contagious qualities came through as prominent features of his sermon delivery (and the way in which God's servant delivers his message speaks worlds about its significance for the herald himself). Owing to the change of medium—from oral delivery to transcriptions from tapes— one aspect of the communicative effectiveness has been removed. Nevertheless, a good measure of the personality, vitality, and wit of the preacher does come through in the rich rhetoric of the sermons.

The most crucial and powerful of these sermons are the first three, which have an altogether different origin. While working with the chapel sermons, I was made aware of a very special set of sermons which Mrs. Caralie Brown had preserved in manuscript form and which shed much light on the perspective, faith, and theology of the other sermons. The Brown family passed through deep waters during 1956 and 1957. They lost their four-year-old son to cancer. During those trying months, they made a covenant not to live a tragedy but to exercise their faith. In keeping that covenant, Dr. Brown preached three very significant sermons, one delivered when they learned that Bryan had cancer ("When God's Love Floods the Heart"), a second which was the funeral sermon for Bryan preached on Good Friday, 1957 (which Ray only entitled "The Funeral Sermon," but which I have here entitled "A Little Child Shall Lead Them," drawing on one of the emphases of the sermon), and a third sermon preached two days later, on Easter, 1957 ("Lift Up Your Hearts!"). The faith which supported and stabilized Ray and Caralie Brown as they went through the valley of the shadow of death remained constant throughout his life. In classroom conversations and lectures, in personal counseling with students and parishioners, and in several of these sermons Ray obviously drew strength and direction from that crisis and victory of twenty years earlier. Mrs. Brown has graciously allowed the use of those three sermons in this volume. Because of their significance for his faith and because of their timeless value for us all, they have been included as a fitting beginning to this collection of his messages.

Owing to the fact that Dr. Brown documented the first three sermons in this collection, editorial alteration there has been minimal. However, the taped sermons required documentation, editorial alterations, and adjustments for the sake of preparing them for print. These sermons were not originally presented with a view to publication. They are presented here not as original creations, but as meditations, exhortations, celebrations, addresses; therefore, they draw from a rich storehouse of ideas, poems, hymns, and memoirs which came to mean so much to Professor Brown personally. Serious effort has been made to locate and give due credit to the sources of the quotations and allusions. Fortunately, the sources of almost all of them were found and have been noted. Frequently, Dr. Brown would give extemporaneous recitations of poetry or striking prose for which the original sources could not be discovered. As a consequence, some beautiful passages and rich illustrations have been deleted where documentation was necessary but impossible. Some of the short maxims or sententious sayings are virtually impossible to document, but have been included, since the introduction to such sayings always gives credit to the proper source by name. No omission of credit has been made purposefully. All Scripture quotations are from the Revised Standard Version, unless another version or a paraphrase is noted.

The title of this book, *The Fire of Truth*, is used for several reasons. First, it was the devotion of Dr. Brown's life to search for and live by God's truth. Second, the theme of kindling devotion on the altar of the heart, being spiritually alive and active for God, found expression in a number of his sermons. As I have been privileged to work closely with these materials during the past months, I have found my own heart warmed and my spirit challenged to greater faithfulness and service for our Lord. All who read these messages will be similarly rewarded.

I should like to thank some generous friends for their

assistance with this volume. First, I owe a large debt of thanks to Mrs. Caralie Brown for providing me with manuscript copies of the sermons in chapters 1 through 3, for her help with manuscript research on the remaining chapters, and for her hearty encouragement in this endeavor. Mrs. Brown has graciously decided that royalties generated by this book will go to the Raymond Bryan Brown Scholarship at Southeastern Baptist Theological Seminary, for the education of young ministers of the gospel. Mr. Ed Sansbury, Director of Audiovisual Services of the Emery B. Denny Library provided immeasurable help in working with the tape recordings of the chapel sermons. Dr. John Carlton, Dr. John I Durham, and Mrs. Mary Lee were most helpful in locating the sources of some of the quotations. Mrs. Evelyn Carter, who typed the manuscript, deserves much credit for its appearance.

Soli Deo Gloria

RICHARD A. SPENCER

1
When God's Love Floods the Heart

More than that, we ought to glory in our troubles, for we know that trouble produces endurance, and endurance, character, and character, hope, and hope will not disappoint us. For, through the holy Spirit that has been given us, God's love has flooded our hearts.

(Romans 5:3-5, Goodspeed)

We ought to glory in our troubles. That is what Paul wrote to the Christians at Rome. But how can we glory in our troubles? And why should we exult in those experiences which bring grief and heartbreak and doom to our tender hearts? Do we rejoice in our troubles just to be brave, or to be martyrs, or to call attention to ourselves, or because we refuse to face life seriously?

We should glory in our troubles, Paul declares, because trouble produces endurance. That is, it gives us the power to withstand difficulty. It helps us bow our necks and backs and accept what comes to us. It is the power to fight to the bitter death rather than give in.

There are soldiers who are proud of their endurance, having been trained to suffer rigor and torture rather than

A sermon preached on July 29, 1956 at Tabernacle Baptist Church in Richmond, Virginia, after learning that the Browns' four-year-old son, Raymond Bryan Brown, Jr., had cancer.

betray their native land. In time there comes to them a strength which is endurance. When troubles come to us they slowly create within us the capacity to withstand, the power to endure. One who must go through deep waters thrusts his feet firmly upon whatever footings he can, steadies himself, and keeps walking, walking, head front, to the other side! And, though the waters roll over him, the waves do not overwhelm him.

We can declare, furthermore, that the endurance which trouble brings us who belong to Christ has the power to transform evil into good. Nowhere is this revealed with greater power than in the life of our Lord himself.

> Christ also suffered for you, leaving you an example, that you should follow in his steps. He committed no sin; no guile was found on his lips. When he was reviled, he did not revile in return; when he suffered, he did not threaten; but he trusted to him who judges justly. He himself bore our sins in his body on the tree, that we might die to sin and live to righteousness. By his wounds you have been healed.[1]

His sufferings, his trials, and his tribulations brought us our salvation. Does it not bring quiet to that storm in your own troubled soul to understand that *your* sufferings, yes, *yours,* can make God near and dear to others who need a balm in Gilead?

My friends, our sufferings can never be destroyed, but they can be overcome. How? When we use them to testify to the goodness and glory of God! In those last agonizing hours when he awaited his approaching death, Jesus cried out, "Now is my soul troubled. And what shall I say? 'Father, save me from this hour'? No, for this purpose I have come to this hour. Father, glorify thy name."[2] Ah, these frail hearts of yours and mine, almost lost in defeat, are victorious over sorrow when God in Christ is triumphant over the despond of the soul!

This patient endurance which trouble fashions for us is also the quality that keeps us on our feet with our faces to the wind. When George Matheson was stricken blind and disappointed in love, he prayed that he might accept God's will, "not with dumb resignation, but with holy joy; not only with the absence of murmur, but with a song of praise."[3] The shrill winds and pouring rain are helpless in the face of a man like that! Why should we glory in our troubles? Because troubles produce endurance. "Rejoice always, pray constantly, give thanks in all circumstances; for this is the will of God in Christ Jesus for you."[4]

We ought to rejoice in our troubles because, declared a man who ought to know, endurance produces character. Experience produces character, and character reveals experience. Our character depends upon our transformation of our experience.

When Paul spoke of "character" he meant the capacity to withstand stress and strain. We often declare that a person has character when he is not easily moved by mishap or misfortune, or when he has the flexibility to bend with circumstances and not be broken. Such a soul has been tested in the trials of life and can withstand the battle. Anyone who lives this life of ours needs character like that! For, "If you have raced with men on foot, and they have wearied you, how will you compete with horses? And if in a safe land you fall down, how will you do in the jungle of the Jordan?"[5]

If you cannot face the little things of life, this noble prophet of God was crying, how can you face the things that can tear and shatter and rend your souls? Character is the capacity to withstand stress and strain. Weak? Yes! Tired?

Yes! Cast down? Yes! Unsteady? Yes! Stumbling? Yes! Destroyed? Not that soul who clings to Christ!

But we must go on. Character is also the strength of a man who has deep faith, and keeps a steady course. Again we go for insight to him who is the Lamb of God. "Although he was a Son, *he learned obedience through what he suffered;* and being made perfect he became the source of eternal salvation to all who obey him."[6]

The experience of the divine Son of God helped to make his character. And with the psalmist he could have cried, "The Lord is my light and my salvation; whom shall I fear? The Lord is the refuge of my life; of whom shall I be afraid?"[7] The source of his strength, and ours, is in his heavens still!

We ought to glory in our troubles because, said a man who had seen the blackest night, *character produces hope.*[8] And what is it that you and I mean by hope? We mean, usually, life and not death for the future. We mean happiness and not sorrow for the future. But can life ever really promise us that? Who knows? Who among us will soon find a dream shattered, a home broken, a life diseased and disordered, quicker than lightning flashes in the sky? If we mean by hope an unruffled future we will not have it.

But hope is not hope that hopes for an easy future. Only Christian hope is hope, for it is hope that is grounded in God. So let our hearts be comforted. Let them rejoice! Our hope is in what God has already done for us: "God shows his love for us in that while we were yet sinners Christ died for us."[9] "O soul in distress out on life's sea, know that he came to us and for one purpose alone, to save us! Never forget, almost two thousand years ago, the Most High gave *us* the Lamb of God. By his advent, Christ sets within our reach the hope that never terminates because it terminates our hopelessness."[10]

Our hope, moreover, is in the meaning Christ gives it. It all goes back to that first Easter day when a dead Jesus appeared as the living Christ. And one who knew him cried out triumphantly for all the household of faith for all the centuries, "Blessed be the God and Father of our Lord Jesus Christ! In his great mercy he has caused us to be born anew to a life of hope through Jesus Christ's resurrection from the dead."[11] Let our hearts be glad! Upon this knowledge—Christ is risen—our faith is built and, because of this faith, we have hope, confidence in the power of God. We have a future because Christ had a past!

Hope for those who belong to Christ means that God can be trusted. Does it mean that questioning will not come? Does it mean that hurt will not come? Does it mean that sorrow will not come? No, but thanks be to God it *does* mean that the word of the Lord is true.

> When through the deep waters I call thee to go,
> The rivers of woe shall not thee overflow;
> For I will be with thee thy troubles to bless,
> And sanctify to thee thy deepest distress.[12]

Only Christian hope like this allows a man to face life with steady eyes.

Most of all, our hope is fellowship with God, which begins even now to transform us and our world into the likeness of the Son of God, and which, at the end of this life, will grow and grow in the greatness of God our Father. We have hope for the future because God's Spirit possesses us in the present. We are prisoners of an everlasting hope! We see not just today or tomorrow but tomorrow and tomorrow and forever! The church of Christ is the fellowship of the last day. And we are willing to wait because we wait for the Lord!

Hope, Paul cries out, never disappoints us. Why? How? Because, he continues—and mark these blessed words— "God's love has flooded our hearts."[13] Pierced and bleeding, beating fast or slow, these hearts of ours are running over with the love of God! There is a bleak hill outside a city wall. And a man on a cross who died to save us all! He has "[opened] now the crystal fountain,/Whence the healing waters flow."[14]

And now we are confident that nothing happens to us outside God's love. "In the world you have tribulation; but be of good cheer, I have overcome the world."[15] These are the words of the Lord. The apostle Paul wrote for *us,* "We know that in everything God works for good with those who love him, who are called according to his purpose."[16] Nothing happens to us outside the love of God.

Nothing can separate us from the love of God. In the Book of Daniel three young men were thrown into a fiery furnace because of their devotion to God. They were being called upon not so much to withstand fire as to hold on to God. In the midst of the ordeal, King Nebuchadnezzar said, "I see four men quite free, walking in the middle of the fire, . . . The appearance of the fourth is like an angel!"[17] Burn down deep into your soul, my friend, the faith and the words of one we can trust:

> For I am sure that neither death, nor life, nor angels,
> nor principalities, nor things present, nor things to
> come, nor powers, nor height, nor depth, nor any-
> thing else in all creation, will be able to separate us
> from the love of God in Christ Jesus our Lord.[18]

Have you ever been in a dark cave in the blackest of night when there was no light, not a glimmer of light at all? Has the darkness that surrounded you pulled in every direction, silently waiting to drop you from the narrow rim into a bottomless pit of despair in which you would never stop falling? And were you afraid to move, but unable to keep still? But at last you must walk. Slowly now. Slowly. And then—and then—in a moment your heart is flooded with something very great. You walk surely now and with steady pace. And you are not afraid anymore. Yonder! Yonder ahead you see a light. At times it is very near to give you heart. Again it is far away to lead you on through the darkness. Be not afraid. It is the Lord! And, by the mercies of God, you know that we ought to rejoice in our troubles because "God's love has flooded our hearts."[19]

2
A Little Child Shall Lead Them

Today, as we gather in the house of God, our thoughts are here and in a distant place. Long, long ago a man gave his life at this hour for a world, for all the worlds that be. Today, in this solemn hour, our hearts are made to rejoice because he died that we might live. The comfort so gentle and tender in our hearts to sustain us, and the living hope that beckons us—Oh bless his name!—they come to us from *him*!

In the long and uneasy days that have slipped away, my wife and I have learned together in the bonds of human love and in the bonds of Christ. *Suffering and sorrow have taught us the height of human joy and the depth of human suffering.* How much we learned from a life of four years! (So much more it seems to me than I ever learned from life *apart* from him.) How truly the ancient prophet spoke when he declared, "A little child shall lead them."[1] Radiance and laughter and devotion—these we came to know in all their fullness. What are these things? They are what we learned from *him*!

What it means to want to bear the suffering of others we learned, too, from him. This has taught us most of all about the Lord we serve, because "Only suffering trains for

This funeral sermon for Raymond Bryan Brown, Jr., was delivered on Good Friday, April 19, 1957.

18

eternity; for eternity rests in faith, but faith is in obedience, and obedience is learned from suffering."[2] That sensitive soul was right who said that "the schooling for life shows its results in time, but the life-school of suffering trains for eternity."[3]

Suffering and sorrow have also taught us the overarching and undergirding love of God. Long ago Samuel Rutherford spoke for *us* when he wrote, "Tears have a tonge (sic.) and grammar and language that our father knoweth."[4] And there is that comforting word of the Lord declared to the prophet, "Fear not: for I have redeemed thee, I have called thee by thy name; thou art mine. When thou passest through the waters, I will be with thee; and through the rivers, they shall not overflow thee."[5] How often have our hearts been kept by God's promise to the apostle Paul, "My grace is sufficient for thee."[6]

One day, in the months that are passed, as I rode along the road, thinking about our son, I breathed as a prayer some words from a hymn I dearly love, "[O may I] never, never/Outlive my love to Thee!"[7] There came to me that day, as if from a Living Voice, the words, "Thou shalt never, never outlive my love of thee!" I was comforted. He who belongs to Christ is never called to take any journey on which he will find himself forsaken. "Let not your heart be troubled . . . . I will not leave you orphans."[8]

I do not know how much of life God sends us. I am not certain about how much he wills for us. But I know that whatever comes to us, he wills to help us bear it and he yearns to bring us through! He does not leave us forsaken but enters into our feeble lives and empowers us by his Spirit. Baron von Hügel, one of the great Christians of our time, once wrote, "Christ came, and He did not really explain it [suffering]; He did far more, He met it, willed it, transformed it, and He taught us how to do all this, or rather He Himself does it within us, if we do not hinder the all-healing hands."[9]

We learn, too, that he who gives to us gives only to take away. But he who takes away does so only to give again—as only the God of our Lord Jesus can! John Bunyan relates in *The Pilgrim's Progress* the day Christian and Hopeful came to the River of Death. Upon entering the waters, "Christian began to sink, and crying out to his good friend Hopeful, he said, I sink in deep Waters; the Billows go over my head, all his Waves go over me . . . Then said the other, Be of good cheer my Brother, I feel the bottom, and it is good."[10]

The love of God is broader than the measure of men's minds. And how do we learn this? We cannot get over our sorrow, but we can get into it; and, when we do, we see the face of one full of sorrows and acquainted with grief, who understands us and undergirds us with the love of God.[11] Our faith in his love is made strong. "When human wisdom cannot see a hand's breadth before it in the dark night of suffering, then faith can see God, for faith sees best in the dark."[12]

Suffering and sorrow have taught us, too, that we must live life with our eyes set on eternity. We must live eternally in the present hour, in company with Jesus Christ. We are, as the Book of Hebrews expresses it, "strangers and pilgrims on the earth."[13] It is within our Christian faith that we learn to declare with Paul,

> For our light affliction, which is for the moment, worketh for us more and more exceedingly an eternal weight of glory; while we look not at the things which are seen, but at the things which are not seen: for the

things which are seen are temporal; but the things which are not seen are eternal.[14]

In *The Pilgrim's Progress,* we find Christian about to cross a narrow path over a deep, dark chasm. Fearing, he hesitates. Then he hears a voice out of the darkness, "Though I walk through the Valley of the Shadow of Death, I will fear none ill, for thou art with me."[15] Here is the story of our pilgrimage—my wife's and mine—through this life in the life of Christ. It is not easy to walk the earth looking down in the dark. There comes a time when we can walk most surely upon the ground by looking at the stars. We have looked up and heard his voice; we hear him say now, "Come straight to me and you will be all right."

We cannot go around suffering, but we can go through it. The way winds to a hill called Calvary and through an empty tomb and ends at the right hand of God. All the glory of Easter is ours today on this Good Friday! We give up those whom we love not to death but to a living Christ! The Son of God has been raised from the dead, the first fruits of those who have fallen asleep. "There is in life one blessed joy: to follow Christ; and in death one last blessed joy: to follow Christ to life!"[16]

One July day when the world was full of gloom and there was no light at all, I read at the end of the day, as I always do, from a book of devotions. I shall always believe that the words I read that day were the gift of God. A good man wrote these words:

> You must accustom yourself more and more to the thought that here is not our abiding city, that all that we call ours here is only lent, not given us, and that if the sorrow for those we have lost remains the same,

we must yet acknowledge with gratitude to God the
blessing of having enjoyed so many years with those
whom He gave us as parents or children or friends.[17]

In loving gratitude and in holy faith we now give up our
son; not to death, but a living Christ! There will be a bright
tomorrow—our Lord Jesus will bring it.

When the day that he [Mr. Valiant] must go hence was
come, many accompanied him to the River-side, into
which as he went he said, Death, where is thy sting? and
as he went down deeper he said, Grave, where is thy
Victory? So he passed over, and all the Trumpets
sounded for him on the other side.[18]

Bless the Lord, O my soul: and all that is within me,
bless his holy name![19]

*O God our Father, who alone loses none dear to thee, what
is nearer to thee than a confessing heart and a life of faith?
Thanks be to thee, who sent thy Son to give us life that none
can take away. Remind us never to look for life in the land of
death. Rather, teach us that there is no death in the land of
life. Grant that we shall dread nothing but the loss of thee.
Keep us close to thy Son, and the love that has borne with us
and the heart that suffers for us. Through Christ our Lord,
who liveth and reigneth with thee, One God, world without
end. Amen.*

3
Lift Up Your Hearts!

Mary stood sobbing outside the tomb. . . . "Mary!"
said Jesus. . . . Away went Mary of Magdala to the
disciples with the news, "I have seen the Lord!"
(John 20:11,16,18, Moffatt)

Most of us like a sad story if it has a happy ending.
Tragedy sometimes is a goodly medicine for our minds and
hearts; if a tragedy is turned into a happy story, and if a
defeat is turned into a victory, we like it. The first Easter
seemed to be only the third day after a terrible calamity.
And life was a dreary business, to be lived with tired steps
and dull eyes and smashed hearts. On this present glorious
day of hope and joy and life let us go back, more than
nineteen centuries, to Jerusalem.

There we are among them, those folk who were so sad!
Shock and surprise and bewilderment and numbness
jammed into desolate hearts. Heads could not be lifted up,
and knees could not stand. Little wonder! *They felt that
they had lost their world.* And theirs was a big world to
lose. It had been in the making for centuries. Prophets had
foretold it. Sages had taught it. The poor cherished it. The
learned debated it. The sorrowful were gladdened by it.

A sermon preached on Easter, April 21, 1957, two days after Bryan's
funeral.

23

The joyful were thankful for it. Ah, blessed Jesus! He had enlarged their world, for he put more of heaven into it.

New hopes he had brought, and new insights, too. They were hopes of an eternal fellowship of life in God for all who sought his presence and insights that in him there was "no East or West, In him no South or North." Hopes and insights—gone!

New convictions he had brought, and a new allegiance, too. He it was who should be the Redeemer of his people. Had he not boldly proclaimed it? And had they not followed him over hills and valleys and along dusty roads because he would lead them in at heaven's gate? Convictions and allegiance—gone!

Jesus had destroyed their world, for both heaven and earth were gone. When dreams built upon truth are shattered, then the world is gone!

They were certain that they had lost their dearest friend. But still they could cherish his memory. Back to the Sea of Galilee and lepers healed and blind men seeing and lame men walking. Back to the lilies of the field and the birds of the air, which were cares of God. Back to the kingdom of God, which men entered and by which they were held.

There were words that he had spoken: "Fear not, little flock, for it is your Father's good pleasure to give you the kingdom." "Do you think that I cannot appeal to my Father, and he will at once send me more than twelve legions of angels?"[1] But at the end of it all:

> O sacred Head, now wounded,
> With grief and shame weighed down,
> Now scornfully surrounded
> With thorns, Thine only crown.[2]

Yet they pondered his meaning for their lives in the

midst of their grief. "Our own hope was that he would be the redeemer of Israel; but he is dead, and that is three days ago!"[3]

And they performed loving deeds for him. At early dawn some women from Galilee took spices that they had prepared and went to the tomb. (With what reverence and tenderness sorrowful hearts place flowers upon a grave!) These were the souls who, along with others, watched him die, standing at a distance. "Language thou art too narrow, and too weake to ease us now; great sorrow cannot speake."[4] Wonder and sorrow and confusion were in their souls.

> Who was this one of whom the ages tell,
>> The lowly Peasant come from Nazareth,
>> And yet who knew the words of life and death?
> He came all hope into our earthly hell;
> But men, poor dwellers in the nature-shell,
>> Saw not that He had come to set them free:
>> He was too great for their hearts: they could not see
> He drew his water from a higher well.[5]

But this was not all. *The disciples of Jesus, we can imagine, were afraid that they had lost their own hearts.* They could no longer live with themselves. They were not the same any more, for they had lost their most precious possession, the friend of sinners. It is not easy for a man to live with only part of himself, and all who are dear to us are a part of us.

More than this, they had lost respect for themselves for believing what they did. They would be pointed out by those who would laugh and scorn: "You were with the Nazarene too, with Jesus!" Forgive all of them who felt like crying out, "If thou be Christ save thyself and us." For if their hearts were like ours they were wont to cry: "My God, my God, why hast thou forsaken us!"

They were lost! People are lost who do not know where they belong. And the disciples did not know where they were or where to go or how to go. Yet they knew one thing: they would go back to the past that had no new world and held no dear friend. All of this is in the desolate word of Peter: "I go a-fishing."[6]

The followers of the man from Galilee had forgotten one thing: the God and Father of our Lord Jesus Christ! There was the testimony of Jesus that his was the God of the living and not the dead. And there was his sure word, "I am not alone, for the Father is with me."[7] There was the steadying reminder, "Be of good cheer, I have overcome the world."[8] Here was the promise of the Son which was meant to bring strength and courage and victory.

Suddenly he was in their midst—alive! The dead Jesus now the living Lord! He comes—the message of Easter— triumphant over the grave when everything is lost. He comes—when sorrow is the heaviest! He comes—when destruction is the greatest! He comes—and salvation is the nearest! Hear him speak to every disciple in every age: When your world comes to an end, I will come to you. When catastrophe engulfs you, I will enfold you. When your heads are bowed in sorrow, lift up your hearts in joy!

The word he reveals is the one word we long to hear: those who belong to Christ will live! "We say, 'In the midst of life we die.' God answers, 'Nay, in the midst of death we live.'"[9] Death is our enemy and would be to the end. But Christ comes! When he guards us and keeps us, he transforms death from defeat into victory, from despair into hope, from destruction into completion. "The death which they thought to inflict on Him as dishonour and disgrace has become the glorious monument to death's defeat."[10] So—bless his name—death becomes not the end but the beginning. It is not the end of the way, but the way of the beginning. For Christ brought the end of death and the beginning of Life!

And let all our frail and needy hearts remember that at Eastertime Christ finds those who need him most. He stands *this* Easter Day and calls us by name as he called Mary that first glad day in the long ago. Forgiving our sins and offering us life, he finds us. The disciples had lost their friend, but their lost friend found *them*—and does still! We are able to find ourselves because God finds *us*. We could never reach up to God, but he has already reached down to us. This is the gladsome news of Easter!

So, lift up your hearts! Hope for the future lies in what God did long ago when he raised Christ triumphant from the grave. And the Spirit of God abides in our hearts in this present hour to empower us and to assure us: there will be a last day, a Great Day of the Lord, for all who are kept in Christ's hand. So, lift up your hearts! "If you have heard the Easter message, you can no longer run around with a tragic face and lead the humourless existence of a man who has no hope."[11]

When trouble steals upon you, sing "He's got the whole wide world in His hand." When night comes, pray "Lead, kindly Light! amid th' encircling gloom." When there is no place to stand, sing "How firm a foundation, ye saints of the Lord!" And when there is no abiding city, remember "Jerusalem, the golden,/With milk and honey blest!"

Be possessed of Christ, and you will know that through the tender mercy of God the dayspring from on high has visited us, to give light to them that sit in darkness and in the shadow of death and to guide our feet into the way of peace.

In the midst of our days and years Christ confronts us as surely as he did his sorrowing disciples long ago. And, Lord of life, he cries: I *died* and I *live* for you!

"Lift up your hearts!"
We lift them, Lord, to Thee;
Here at Thy feet none other may we see;
"Lift up your hearts!"
Even so, with one accord,
We lift them up, we lift them to the Lord.[12]

4
How Lovely
Is Thy Dwelling Place

How lovely is thy dwelling place,
O Lord of hosts!
My soul longs, yea, faints
   for the courts of the Lord;
my heart and flesh sing for joy
   to the living God.

Even the sparrow finds a home,
   and the swallow a nest for herself,
   where she may lay her young,
at thy altars, O Lord of hosts,
   my King and my God.
Blessed are those who dwell in thy house,
   ever singing thy praise! Selah

Blessed are the men whose strength is in thee,
   in whose heart are the highways to Zion.
As they go through the valley of Baca
   they make it a place of springs;
   the early rain also covers it with pools.
They go from strength to strength;
   the God of gods will be seen in Zion.

O Lord God of hosts, hear my prayer;
   give ear, O God of Jacob! Selah

A chapel meditation presented on September 1, 1965.

Behold our shield, O God;
   look upon the face of thine anointed!

For a day in thy courts is better
   than a thousand elsewhere.
I would rather be a doorkeeper in the house of my God
   than dwell in the tents of wickedness.
For the Lord God is a sun and shield;
   he bestows favor and honor.
No good thing does the Lord withhold
   from those who walk uprightly.
O Lord of hosts,
   blessed is the man who trusts in thee!
         (Psalm 84:1-12)

The other day, I did something I had not done for a long
time—I read from the Old Testament! And it is remarkable
that we find there abundant spiritual feasts! Surely the
psalm read this morning is precisely this. It is a lesson in
what God's house means to the children of God.

"How lovely is thy dwelling place,/O Lord of hosts!"
These are the words of a man who has learned the meaning
of the worship of God in his Temple. Perhaps the writer of
this psalm had returned from a service of praise in
Jerusalem. Possibly he was far away from his spiritual altar
and longed once more to join the festal throng at the
Temple. What is most important is not the circumstances
surrounding his words, but the reality of his words. They
tell what the house of God in God's city means to the
faithful. "The Lord loveth the gates of Zion more than all
the dwellings of Jacob. Glorious things are spoken of thee,
O city of God."[1]

From the psalmist we learn first of all that the house of
God teaches us where we belong: "My soul longs, yea faints

for the courts of the Lord; . . . " And the words follow closely upon these, "my heart and flesh sing for joy to the living God." God is real to the psalmist in his tabernacle and among his people. When the psalmist meets God in the Temple, he meets also his neighbor. And when he meets his neighbor in the Temple, he meets God. In God's house, the psalmist is at home. How well Walter Rauschenbusch expressed the reality of the spiritual life when he wrote,

> When I enter into God,
> All life has a meaning,
> Without asking I know; . . .
> When I am in him, I am in the Kingdom of God
> And in the Fatherland of my Soul.[2]

Secondly, it is in God's house of worship that the man of faith learns that he belongs. We belong together, God, neighbor, and I. And the worship of God sets forth this reality known only through the grace of God. When we are where we belong, we know that we belong to God and to each other. If the ancient pilgrims marched together to Zion because of a covenant in the desert, what shall those pilgrims do because of a covenant, "Without a city wall,/ Where the dear Lord was crucified,/Who died to save us all"?[3] The crucified and risen Lord is the basis and the goal of our community, and because of his sacrifice we are able to declare with a reality unknown to the psalmist, "How lovely is thy dwelling place,/O Lord of hosts!" We belong together in the worship of God in his house. We will never belong to one another unless we belong to God. And we belong to each other because we belong to Christ. When we put ourselves where we belong, we learn that we belong.

My fervent prayer as we begin a new year together is that we will learn that we belong in a community of worship and are called to cry with the psalmist, "My heart and flesh sing for joy to the living God."

Dietrich Bonhoeffer, in his touching little book on the church, wrote,

> It is easily forgotten that the fellowship of Christian brethren is a gift of grace, a gift of the Kingdom of God that any day may be taken from us. . . . Therefore, let him who until now has had the privilege of living a common Christian life with other Christians praise God's grace from the bottom of his heart. Let him thank God on his knees and declare: It is grace, nothing but grace, that we are allowed to live in community with Christian brethren.[4]

The psalmist teaches us that we who are brethren because we have sensed God's grace belong in his house, singing for joy to the living God with the family of God. Even as the swallows find a nesting place in the providence of God, so the man of God finds his abiding place at the altar of God.

The psalmist teaches us in our lesson today, also, that in God's house we learn what is ours. In the fellowship of the faithful and in the Temple, people of faith find strength for pilgrimage. "Blessed are the men whose strength is in thee, . . . They go from strength to strength." Through the reality of God known in worship, men can turn weakness into strength and hardship into opportunity. The bleak places of life hold no despondency for pilgrims who, in the words of Artur Weiser, "are carried along as if they had invisible wings, so that the way of faith becomes a walking on high mountains leading from one peak to another."[5] The psalmist teaches us that the God who meets us at his altar leads us to it, and the strength for the journey to heaven's gate comes from the Lord of hosts, our King and God.

Once more, we who here today possess the vitality that is known through the God and Father of our Lord Jesus Christ can claim the word of Paul as our own, "I can do all things through Christ who strengthens me."[6] And our praise should exceed the psalmist's. In God's house and in worship with the faithful, men find strength for the journey.

This last spring I visited the great locks at Muscle Shoals, Alabama. While there, I observed how a large barge covered with steel was locked into position in one of the locks. Massive gates were drawn and tons of water rushed beneath it. Slowly and quietly, the barge began to rise. And, after a while, on an entirely different level, it made its journey up the river. It was placed on a new level because it was locked into position so that it could receive a lift it could not give itself. In worship we lock ourselves into position so that we will be able to receive the quiet strength of God.

Life is full of desert places like the valley of Baca. Dry and barren land it was that had to be crossed before Zion could be seen gleaming in the distance. Yes, life is full of wastelands, spiritual wastelands, and there seems to be no water at times to soothe a parched tongue and no rain to make flowers grow. "But," says the psalmist, "those who possess God's strength go through the valley of Baca and make it a place of springs."[7]

Dr. Harold Bosley, pastor of the First Methodist Church in Evanston, Illinois, told of a meeting in a Negro church which he attended during his student days at the University of Chicago during the Depression. Clarence Darrow was one of the featured speakers. So was Charles Gilkey, the dean of the chapel at the University of Chicago. There were several others who spoke. And in the midst of his oration, in which he summed up the woes of the Negroes, Darrow satirically asked, "What do you have to sing about?" And Bosley said one of the Negro women in the congregation shouted, "We've got Jesus to sing about!"[8] God's pilgrims go through the valley of Baca and make it a place of springs.

And not only is strength given for the pilgrimage. There is the gift of direction and vision. "Blessed are the men . . . in whose heart are the highways to Zion . . . the God of gods will be seen in Zion." The hearts of men are not very large, but all kinds of highways lead away from them. The psalmist praises the man whose heart makes the journey to Zion. The man who turns to worship God is the man who returns to worship God. He finds at God's altar the direction to the heavenly Zion. And he nurtures his experience because the God of gods will be seen in Zion.

We who are gathered here this morning may need some roadwork done on our roads to Zion. We may need the roadbuilder to repair, with his strong and loving hands, those paths in our hearts that lead to his throne. We need the direction and vision of his will to make them the kinds of roads that bring us, with life transformed, into the endless service of praise and thanksgiving of God.

Let us not despair this morning if our roads do not all lead to Zion. Let us come to his house. And perhaps we will learn that he has brought us here, and has quietly set us upon the way of unbounded joy and unspeakable praise to God the Father. We need only remember that none need enter here who knows no need.

The psalmist teaches us, last of all, whose we are. "O Lord of hosts, blessed is the man who trusts in thee!" "Behold, our shield, O God; look upon the face of thine anointed!" How deep is the reality of God to the psalmist.

"For a day in thy courts is better than a thousand else-where./I would rather be a doorkeeper in the house of my God than dwell in the tents of wickedness." God is so real to him that he prefers to be just outside the house of God than to be inside the house of wickedness. Life with men in the world cannot be compared with life with God in his Temple. "A day in thy courts is better than a thousand elsewhere."

The Lord knows that the faithful are his. "For the Lord God is a sun and shield; he bestows favor and honor. No good thing does the Lord withhold from those who walk uprightly." And the faithful know that they are God's. When Martin Luther found himself without political and religious protection before the authorities in the Roman Church, he took his shelter under the broad shield of Almighty God. This is the kind of faith to which the psalmist invites us.

In God's house we learn to walk uprightly before him and our neighbor. At the altar of God we learn that the God to whom we belong blesses those who walk uprightly. And to walk uprightly is to honor God and to love one another.

Such lessons did we learn from the psalmist. As we begin a year of study together, let it be, too, a year of worship together. As we exercise the mind, let us exercise, too, the heart. As we enthrone Christ in our minds, let us place him, too, on the altars of our hearts. Let us come often to this place and make it our Zion. Let us come not because of our worthiness, but because of our unworthiness. Let us come not because we are spiritually rich, but because we are spiritually poor. Let us come not because of our words, but because of his Word. Let us come because of the great gift of Christ who is our gospel. "How lovely is thy dwelling place, O Lord of hosts." May God mercifully grant to you and me this year that as we meet in chapel we shall hear church bells, because the rope is pulled by the hand of God. Let us pray.

O God our Father, who has blessed our coming in, bless our going forth. And though we leave thy house, may we not leave thee. Through Christ our Lord. Amen.

5
Remember Jesus Christ

Holy Father, we come to thee because thou hast come to us. Thou hast taught us to seek thy face; and we bow before the God whose glory we have seen in the face of Christ. How can we live apart from thee? Teach us that life is redeemed only in thee. Forgive us today of all that thwarts thy will in our lives. Renew us by the cleansing of thy forgiveness and the fullness of thy mercies. Enable us by the power of thy Spirit and the tranquillity of thy peace. Teach us to seek thy counsel in all our needs, that our lives may show forth thy praise. Gather to thyself in love all whom we hold dear and all who are dear to thee, that the world in which we live may reflect indeed the glory of thy grace. Hear our prayer through Jesus Christ our Lord. Amen.

Remember Jesus Christ, risen from the dead, descended from David, as preached in my gospel, the gospel for which I am suffering and wearing fetters like a criminal. But the word of God is not fettered. Therefore I endure everything for the sake of the elect, that they also may obtain salvation in Christ Jesus with its eternal glory.
(2 Timothy 2:8-10)

Several months ago, I talked with a man who kept saying to me, "I can't remember." Even though the questions

A chapel meditation presented on January 19, 1966.

pointed only to yesterday, he could not recall. In old age and sickness, he had lost one of humanity's most precious gifts, memory. He had forgotten many things that would have troubled him or brought him sorrow or anxiety. But he had lost, too, the treasury of beautiful memories with its light and joy.

Memory is vital to meaningful human existence. Israel long ago was admonished to remember the mighty works of God: "Remember that you were a servant in the land of Egypt, and the Lord your God brought you thence with a mighty hand and an outstretched arm."[1] In matters of faith in God, memory is a precious gift. It revives faith. It brings renewal. It conveys reality. Through memory we make the past our contemporary.

"Remember Jesus Christ, risen from the dead." Our Lord belongs to the world beyond us. Let this be reality in the heart of faith. The one crucified with a crown of thorns possesses a crown of diadems. Earth's rejected has become God's accepted. His resurrection marks God's victory in his death. More than anything else, I suppose, Easter is a story about God. It tells what he can do with a grave. "We say," says Luther, "'In the midst of life we die.' God answers, 'Nay, in the midst of death we live.'"[2] Christ's resurrection from the grave also sets out our assurance of victory over the grave. Here, Adolf Schlatter once observed, is the birthplace of life eternal.

Faith knows, too, that Christ's resurrection is the beginning of present spiritual realities for all who have trustful hearts. The petty pace of life is quickened because· we realize that we have been raised to new life in him. What Elizabeth Barrett Browning said of one very dear to her, we say of him:

> The face of all the world is changed, I think,
> Since first I heard the footsteps of thy soul.[3]

He belongs to the world beyond us; but he gained access to that world by traveling through ours.

Men of faith do not look down into a grave, but up into the world of our Father's presence. To remember that Christ lives with the Father revives our faith, brings renewal of spirit, and conveys reality to the soul.

> Lives again our glorious King, . . .
> Where, O Death, is now thy sting?[24]

"Remember Jesus Christ, . . . descended from David." Our Lord belongs to our world. His history is testimony that he has truly entered into our existence. The poetry of Christmas portrays this at its very heart. He bears with my humanity because he has borne it.

Christ's history is evidence, too, that God sums up the divine purpose in history in our Lord's history. He was David's son, flesh of our flesh, but for our sin. The hopes and fears of all the years were met in him. The ancestral hope had become a presence in the man from Nazareth. His history is proclamation that in him is the fullness of divine revelation. Robert Oppenheimer once said that the best way to send an idea is to wrap it up in a person. God has sent us more than an idea; he has sent us himself in the Son of David. His history is the end of the old world and the beginning of the new, because the beginning of the end has begun in him. Life in this world can never be the same since he has lived among us. Life for us is lighted up with a thousand flares set down in the darkness of the world. Our Lord belongs to our world. To remember this revives our faith, brings renewal of spirit, and conveys reality to the soul.

"Remember Jesus Christ, . . . as preached in my

gospel." Our Lord is present in our preaching. What a staggering thought to possess and beset the soul. The gospel is God's action, the expression of his will and purpose. It is the proclamation of the realization of his intention. The gospel is God in action in Jesus Christ. The word of the church is the word spoken in Christ, who is God's act of grace: "We are ambassadors for Christ, God making his appeal through us."[5] He to whom witness is borne is present in our preaching. Our proclamation becomes the revelation of the revelation of Jesus Christ. God speaks his word through our words. We do not meet living men with dead words. We meet dead men with living words. The gospel is not the recalling of dead words written on the page of a book. It is calling forth the living word written on the heart of God. Through God's grace, in the gospel men hear not words about God; they hear God.

"Remember Jesus Christ, . . . as preached in my gospel." To speak of "my gospel" is not to speak of a private possession but of an inner reality. It is my gospel when I am possessed by it, when I have appropriated its benefits. God's gospel is not real to me until it is mine; and my gospel is no gospel unless it is his. Our Lord is present in our preaching. To remember this revives our faith, brings renewal of spirit, and conveys reality to the soul.

This year is yet very young, and so is this term. We will yet fail him miserably in our mission. We will be unworthy of him in our inner life and in our life with others. We will break his law and stand guilty before him. But let us remember this word. It will deliver us from all the principalities and powers that would undo us: "Remember Jesus Christ."

6
There Is No Prison for the Word of God

Never forget "Jesus Christ risen from the dead, descended from David"—according to my gospel, for which I have to suffer imprisonment as if I were a criminal. (But there is no prison for the word of God.)

(2 Timothy 2:8-9, Moffatt)

In recent months, doors of prisons have swung open and captives have gone free. One looks with an understanding heart at pictures of prisoners embracing those whom they love, free to walk again, held no longer by high walls and strong bars. The writer of the text before us knew quite well that there are prisons in this world that bind and restrain the children of God. He places before us the apostle Paul who was gripped by the strong chains forged by mighty Rome. "I am suffering," says Christ's great herald, "and wearing fetters like a criminal." And it is perfectly clear that imprisonment was his lot because of his commitment to the gospel. The writer of the text knew quite well that the gospel and suffering go together. Making it clear that heralding Christ exacts a costly price, he made the significant observation, "But there is no prison for the word of God."[1] Let faith remember that God's saving action

A chapel meditation presented on April 1, 1966.

in Jesus Christ cannot be restrained by *any* chains fash-
ioned by the hands of man.

Is this not a thought to ponder? Let us mark well in these
times the failure of the church. Let us confess plainly our
varied sins. Let us set forth clearly our perversion of our
divinely-given mission. There is a lot wrong with us. But
there is a lot right with the gospel.

I will admit that I have great feeling for a statement made
some years ago by Canon Alexander of Saint Paul's Cathe-
dral of London. He said that mathematical measurements
showed that Saint Paul's was moving down Fleet Street at
the rate of one inch every one hundred years! Now that
hardly qualifies as deliberate speed.

John Morley, who edited a daily newspaper in the middle
of the nineteenth century, once asked a young journalist
what his specialty was, and he replied, "Invective!" Invective and criticism are not enough for a prophetic minister.
Serenity of faith and triumph of faith come in part from the
confidence that there is no prison for the word of God. And
we had better remember this when we talk about the
condition of the church.

This is the first lesson found in our text—enemies cannot
imprison the word of God. Forces of all kinds send out
octopus-like arms that would lock us in their steely grip at
the same time we wrestle to loose ourselves from the
tightening vise of yet other forces that would crush the
vitality within us. "For we are not contending against flesh
and blood, but against the principalities, against the powers, against the world rulers of this present darkness,
against the spiritual hosts of wickedness in the heavenly
places."[2] Name all of those enemies of the gospel which
have confronted you and even now seek to chain you, and
hear the mighty affirmation of the text meant just for you,

"There is no prison for the word of God." Restraint of the messenger is not restraint of the gospel.

Now it is truly amazing how many conflicting forces can fall in with each other if they conclude that they can fall out with the preacher. A herald remembers, when prison walls are built around him, that such a prison remains freedom when he recalls that faith *is* freedom. Samuel Rutherford, a Presbyterian minister imprisoned several hundred years ago in Scotland, was placed in a dungeon underground with only a tiny window through which at night he looked up at the stars. He once wrote to a friend that one night Jesus came into his cell and every star shone like a ruby. What made the difference was not that Rutherford got out, but that Jesus got in! Dietrich Bonhoeffer's body never got out of prison, but his spirit did. And he once wrote, in his *Letters from Prison,* "O freedom, long have we sought thee in discipline and in action and in suffering. Dying, we behold thee now, and see thee in the face of God."[3] To keep the faith is to remain free and to experience the glory of the text, that there is no prison for the God of our Lord and Savior Jesus Christ!

Paul was bound in Rome, but he wrote the tender letter of joy to Philippi. John was in exile on Patmos, but he was in the Spirit on the Lord's Day. Luther was in the Wartburg, but he translated the New Testament. Bunyan was in Bedford jail, but he wrote *The Pilgrim's Progress.* "Ah," you say, "but these were great men, and great men do great things." But our text does not speak of what God does with great men, but of what he does with a great gospel! An extraordinary gospel makes extraordinary ordinary men.

There is yet another thought that springs from the word before us—friends of the gospel cannot imprison it. One of the surest signs of the inspiration of the gospel is that it manages to survive its friends. For instance, our various theological formulations must set off all kinds of angelic reaction in the heavenly precincts. Our trouble is that we suppose that the extent of our understanding is the extent of God's truth. Whether we hold zealously to the words of the fourth century, or whether we hold high the torch for some twentieth-century savant, we would do well to remember that it is pretty difficult to stuff God into our private package of theological goodies.

It is also an easy temptation to allow our own spiritual experience to become a prison for the word of God. It is rather difficult to put a spiritual Niagara in a theological teacup.

It is also one of our inspired notions that our churchly formulations that refuse reflection are bosom friends of the word of God. Nowhere in literature is this fallacy more powerfully portrayed than in Dostoevski's *The Grand Inquisitor.* The aged minister of the church threatens to imprison Christ because he violates the formula of ecclesiastical prescription. Isn't that always a subtle temptation with us, to make God's church like our own?

Our salvation lies in our awareness that there is no prison for the word of God. God sustains his word by the power set forth in Jesus our Lord. Henry Sloane Coffin once spoke to a young man regarding the ministry. In responding to the young man's complaint that he would have to believe a lot of things, Coffin told him that he would not have to believe a lot of things but one thing a whole lot, and that thing was Jesus Christ. It was the Master who began his ministry by declaring, "The Spirit of the Lord is upon me, because he has sent me to proclaim release to the prisoners."[4] And the Master continues his ministry through us when men hear through us not our words, but God's, and the chains that bind them drop into the abyss reserved for them.

There are still those who would bind God by binding Jesus. Men will still put him in a tomb and roll heavy stones to bar his exit. But no stones men can roll into position can ever keep him in. Heaven's word always is, "He is risen!" And doors closed by men of little faith will never keep him out. Heaven's word is, "Peace be with you." Thanks be to God, our Lord Jesus always keeps coming out and coming back. And heaven's word comes to us as it did that first Easter, "He is going before you to Galilee; there you will see him."[5] Back to the boats and the nets and the life gathered from the sea. In that world where you live, he will meet you. In that world where you and I live, he will meet us. And when we see him, he will have chains in his hands, broken by the power of his gospel. And you will rejoice in God's word to you, "There is no prison for the word of God."

> Bless the Lord, O my soul;
> and all that is within me,
> bless his holy name![6]

7
The Knowledge of God

Our Father in whom we live and move and have our being, and whom to know is life eternal, grant us this day such purity of heart and strength of purpose that no selfish aim may hinder us from knowing thy will, and no weakness keep us from doing it. In thy light may we see light, and in thy service find perfect freedom. Through Christ our Lord. Amen.

I must confess that I have been intrigued by musing on the prelude listed for this service, Johann Sebastian Bach's "Come, Savior of the Heathen." I wondered, first of all, if this was a reflection upon our entering class. And then I thought, no, this may be a reference to us all. And then— perish the thought—I thought it could just be a reference to the speaker! Seriously, the words of this prelude point us to the awesome realities which are meant to occupy all our years as the servants of God.

John Calvin, that genius of Protestantism, opened his immortal *Institutes of the Christian Religion* with these words:

> Our wisdom, in so far as it ought to be deemed true
> and solid wisdom, consists almost entirely of two

A convocation address presented on September 20, 1967.

parts: the knowledge of God and of ourselves. . . . It is evident that man never attains to a true self-knowledge until he have previously contemplated the face of God, and come down after such contemplation to look into himself.[1]

One day in ancient Israel, the word of the Lord came to Jeremiah. And it is God's word for us today:

Let not the wise man glory in his wisdom, let not the mighty man glory in his might, let not the rich man glory in his riches; but let him who glories glory in this, that he understands and knows me, that I am the Lord who practices steadfast love, justice, and righteousness in the earth; for in these things I delight, says the Lord.[2]

Let us note carefully the word of the prophet. The knowledge of God is not a set of facts or a collection of truths or a basket of ideas or a garland of private experience. It is not speculation or observation or investigation or mystical vision. It is not a body of knowledge that one sifts and refines with the notion that one is arranging the body of divinity.

The theoretical life of the philosopher or the theologian or the mystic is not the key that opens the door to the knowledge of God. The knowledge of God is not so much knowledge of his eternal being as it is his claim upon us. The word of Jeremiah teaches us to know God in the world he loves, where he sets the divine claim for steadfast love, justice, and righteousness in the earth. The knowledge of God is mediated to us in the claim of our neighbor upon us. This is the word not only of Jeremiah but of other stalwart men whose words we read in holy Scripture.

In the pages of human history, in the miseries and

triumphs of men, God reveals who he is and what he requires in what he is doing and in what he calls men to do after him. The word of the prophet is a reminder, is it not, that the knowledge of God cannot be isolated from the world of men. The knowledge of God will be found as we serve God as instruments of his steadfast love, justice, and righteousness in the world.

Nevertheless, the proclamation of Jeremiah is a compelling word to us as we begin a new year of study. The very diligence that will mark our work together requires us to hear it. The knowledge of God, according to biblical faith, is revealed to men in human existence. It is revealed. He who hides himself from us reveals himself to us.

The pages of man's life are marked by tokens of divine life. This message is sounded throughout the Bible. Paul expresses the priority of God's action when he writes to the Galatians, "You have come . . . to be known by God."[3] Let us, then, in this year together, not strive to wrest knowledge from him, but to open our lives to him that he may speak a revealing word to us.

The knowledge of God, we must therefore add, is born of relationship. They know God who belong to him. Knowledge comes to us when we acknowledge his claim upon us, when we accept his revelation as our resurrection. When in community we confess that the Lord is God we become an extension of that fellowship stretching across the centuries that has seen his work in the world. The knowledge of God becomes real only when we bow to his claim upon us and act upon his claim.

Knowledge of God is born out of service to God. We know God not when we stand outside his will and study him but when we stand within his will and serve him. Let us remember that doing the truth leads us to the truth. If knowledge of God is granted to those of us who serve him, it is compelling that we strive to clarify, reflect on, and claim the revelation anew in every generation.

At the end of that last century, Charles Hodge, the president of Princeton Theological Seminary, declared that not one new idea had ever marred the teaching of the faculty during his administration. Surely, biblical faith requires not merely recitation, but renewal. Our minds are not abused in biblical faith; they are channeled. Is it not required of us so to learn the Christian faith that we may communicate it rightly to others? In dwelling upon it, we give ourselves to it, and it gives its vibrant reality to us.

Paul Holmer, professor of theology at Yale, has complained that all too much theological education is undertaken in the "about" mode. That is, we learn about God, when what we need is knowledge of God. In a brilliant book that he wrote a number of years ago, Richard Niebuhr warned us about becoming observers of the Christian faith rather than participants within it.

As we begin the new academic year together, perhaps we need to remember that our labor is not to make God an object of investigation, but to proclaim him as the subject of our commitment. Not mere knowledge about him, but knowledge of him—this is the mission that is set before us.

Let faith be renewed this session with the assurance that the knowledge of God gives a stance to life shot through with the vitality born of a disciplined, maturing faith. By God's grace, our knowledge is enriched and deepened. The knowledge of God has become for us the understanding of Jesus Christ. The word of Jeremiah is understood now in the light of Christ, who said, "No one knows the Father except the Son and any one to whom the Son chooses to reveal him."[4]

Faith in Christ leads to the knowledge of Christ. And the knowledge of Christ is the knowledge of God. Therefore,

Jesus' word recorded in the Gospel of John becomes very dear to us: "If you continue in my word, you are truly my disciples, and you will know the truth, and the truth will make you free."[5] Here are condition and promise. If you will continue, you will know.

Let us draw strength from the word of Jesus and make the journey. Knowing Christ, we will learn what it truly means to stand for steadfast love, justice, and righteousness in the earth.

8
I Am Here
to Serve the Lord

Father of all mercies, we rejoice this day in the knowledge that thou dost come to the hearts of the lowly and dost brighten by thy light the lives of all who receive thee. Thou didst prepare the souls of men in the distant past for the coming of thy glory to earth. So now prepare our minds and hearts, that Christ may dwell in us and ever reign in our hearts as the king of love and prince of peace. For thy name's sake. Amen.

In the sixth month the angel Gabriel was sent by God to a town in Galilee called Nazaret, to a maiden who was betrothed to a man called Joseph, belonging to the house of David. The maiden's name was Mary. The angel went in and said to her, "Hail, O favoured one! the Lord be with you!" At this she was startled; she thought to herself, whatever can this greeting mean? But the angel said to her, "Fear not, Mary, you have found favour with God. You are to conceive and bear a son, and you must call his name Jesus. He will be great, he will be called the Son of the Most High, and the Lord God will give him the throne of David his father; he will reign over the house of Jacob forever, and to his reign there shall be no end." "How can this be?" said Mary to the angel, "I have no husband." The angel answered her, "The holy

A chapel meditation presented on December 15, 1967.

> Spirit will come upon you, the power of the Most
> High will overshadow you; hence, what is born will
> be called holy, Son of God. Look, there is your
> kinswoman Elizabeth! Even she has conceived a son
> in her old age, and she who was called barren is now
> in her sixth month; for with God nothing is ever
> impossible." Mary said, "I am here to serve the
> Lord. Let it be as you have said." Then the angel
> went away. . . . Then Mary said, "My soul magnifies
> the Lord, My spirit has joy in God my Saviour: for he
> has considered the humiliation of his servant. From
> this time forth all generations shall call me blessed,
> for He who is Mighty has done great things for me."
> (Luke 1:26-38,46-49, Moffatt)

This morning God delivers his word to us through the
witness of Mary, the mother of our Lord. The messenger of
God wings his way to Mary and tells her that God needs
her to deliver a message of incarnate love to his people.
"How can this happen?" asks Mary. The word of the angel
comes to her, "God will do it."[1] And then comes the word of
Mary to the angel, "I am here to serve the Lord." It was
then that Mary started singing. She sang of what God
would do as if it were already done. Here is her testimony
blessing the whole world and us at Christmas, "I am here to
serve the Lord." We read in the text that after Mary bowed
her spirit to the divine purpose, the angel left her. God
could depend on Mary.

What is it that Mary teaches us in this lesson? She puts
herself at God's disposal. God says to her, "Mary, I need
you." And Mary answers, "I am here to serve the Lord."
We can, however, easily understand why Mary asks how
she can be the instrument of God for such a divine work.
"How can I do this?" she asks. And God answers, "Mary,

you will not do it. I will." Mary learns that she can do what God asked her to do because God will bring it to pass. It is when she learns that she needs only to respond to God, and not to bring it to pass that she says, "I am here to serve the Lord." Mary takes God at his word. She does not reject it; she acts upon it. She believes God can bring his word to pass. In her song, from which we have read a few verses, she sings of what God does in Jesus to fulfill his hope of redeeming his people.

God still comes at Christmas. His word comes especially to those who are waiting for him, to those who are hoping for him. He comes and asks for their help, as surely as he asked for the help of Mary; not, of course, that they give birth to his Son, but that they proclaim his birth. He asks them to bear the message of what he has done and is doing and will do in the world through the birth of that one child. And when men ask, "How is this possible?" he answers still, "I will do it." Now, as then, he provides the power for the tasks to which he calls the sons of men.

There is a tendency among us, I think, to make Christmas a faraway adventure story which we can read but never really live. But Christmas keeps coming as contemporary as our every confrontation with the gospel. And the lesson of Mary faces us: what do we say when God asks our help to spread his good news upon the earth? What songs rise up within our souls because of our commitment to him? God, creator of heaven and earth, needs you and me.

Karl Barth has said that in the person of Mary, mankind has a part in the Incarnation. Surely, today, we who incarnate his gospel serve the Incarnation. God needed Mary to bring his Son to us. And God needs us to carry his Son to the world.

Let us learn from Mary that the noblest response we can ever make to God is to become channels of his grace. And we can never become channels of his grace until we have become recipients of his grace. He comes to us long before we come to him. But he can open his heart only to those who can open their hearts to him.

God can no longer use Mary and the shepherds and the Wise Men and Peter and James and John to tell his story. But he keeps coming at Christmas, hoping to find others like Mary who will listen to what he has to say and who will see what he can do. He still plants songs in the hearts of people who will say, "I am here to serve the Lord." He still comes and asks for our help.

It cost him to come to us. And it costs us to go to him. We must be prepared, like Mary, to sacrifice earthly security, to miss earthly comforts, and to be content when most committed to the divine. But to pay this price is to receive the greatest of all treasures, to learn as Mary did, what it really means to say that God has come to the disfigured and disordered world of men.

God did not call Mary to do his work but to receive it and proclaim it. Her response was that of humility, faith, and obedience. God does not call you and me to do his work but to receive it and proclaim it. He calls us as he called Mary, to be the channels of his grace. Our obedience becomes a channel by which his grace is communicated to the world. It is a great consolation for us that divine majesty became flesh and blood, but an even greater consolation if we can believe that it happened for us. Surely, if one believed this, the heart would break in a thousand pieces for joy.

God calls us now at Christmas to accept the freedom that consists in openness to his grace. He calls us now at Christmas to enter the freedom of service and the service of freedom. God no longer needs to call Mary, but he still needs you and me. Remember Mary and what she said when God needed her—"I am here to serve the Lord."

> What can I give him
> Poor as I am?
> If I were a shepherd,
> I would give him a lamb,
> If I were a wise man,
> I would do my part, —
> But what can I give him,
> Give my heart.[2]

And now, O Lord, as we leave thy house, grant that we will not leave thee. Thou hast come to us to save us. So we pray thee to deliver us from every evil and every trial that may befall us. In thy mercies, grant us the joy of Christmas and the blessing of gathering again in this place to rejoice in thy light and declare thy salvation. Through Christ our Lord we pray. Amen.

9
Loving God with Heart, Soul, and Mind

O God of our fathers, we rejoice this day in the great mercies with which thou hast sustained us and in the providence that has led us to this hour. We give thee thanks for all who have labored before us to bring us an inheritance that is worthy of the best gifts of sacrificial love we can give to our calling here. May thy Spirit rest upon us as we begin our labors, that our work may be truly thine own. Through Christ our Lord. Amen.

We gather in this place because of the love of God. God's love has brought us here. And our love of God has brought us here. The light of the church begins and ends in the love of God. We are those who share the touch of God's love and know the beckoning providence that sets us upon the great venture of sharing in the unfolding knowledge of God given to men of faith who respond to love with love.

The love of God has brought us here, and the love of God will take us from here, witnesses to the transforming power of the love that compels us and inspires us. We are here because the love of God is behind us and before us. And the task that is set before us together is to grow together in learning and setting forth the love of God revealed, possessed, and proclaimed in Jesus Christ.

In the Gospel of Mark, Jesus tells an inquirer that the

A convocation address presented on September 17, 1968.

56

heart of genuine religion is love of God and neighbor.[1] He quotes passages from the sixth chapter of Deuteronomy and from the nineteenth chapter of Leviticus. The passage from Deuteronomy tells of love of God informed by heart, soul, mind, and strength. And the word from Leviticus tells of love that finds its fulfillment in concern for the neighbor.

We are here today because we have heard in the recesses of our hearts the same word of Jesus spoken so long ago. We are here because we love God and neighbor, feebly perhaps, but we love them. Jesus reminds us in his word in Mark that we must love God with our whole selves— emotion, will, and mind. He teaches us to love the neighbor whom we will love more dearly as we understand ourselves and the neighbor to be the children of God whom God in Christ redeems. It is no pride that brings us here. It is humility before so great a redeemer. It is no self-adulation that brings us here. It is joy born of so great a gift. It is not misplaced confidence that brings us here. It is trust in one who out of weakness can make strength. We are here because of his love which, possessing us, has thrust us forth, heralds of the love that sustains us, teaching us of the wonder of God's grace and inspiring us to tell the old, old story of Jesus and his love.

We come to our task in response to the Lord we love and in obedience to his commandment. To love God and neighbor is for us both invitation and command. To learn what it means to love God and neighbor is the great task of the theological seminary, which is the intellectual center of the life of the church. The exercise of the mind is set by Jesus, in the words to which we have referred, in the context of love.

What is this love that brings us here? It is the quality of life that God has revealed in Jesus Christ. It is life that cares, that spends itself, that inspires, that redeems, that never gives up. It is life that finds its fulfillment in the fulfillment of God's will. It is life that gives because it is received, the gift of God's Son. We love because he first loved us.

What is the love that calls for the exercise of all there is of a man—emotion, will, and mind? Richard Niebuhr, the late Yale theologian, said that love is the directing of one's self joyously and unreservedly toward the loved one, that genuine love finds elation in the well-being of the beloved, and does not seek to change him but gives wholehearted acceptance and support to the beloved and what he represents. This means that in loving God, we must also love what he represents and what he is doing in the world.[2]

Now, surely, this great theologian has reminded us that love requires all there is of a man, since such love is directed toward the Creator and Redeemer known in Jesus Christ. And who is my neighbor whom I am to love as myself? Niebuhr suggested that he is the person in whose suffering and need I should see the Suffering Servant.[3]

Surely this neighbor requires all the love there is in a man. If we love God with all of the means that he has given us for loving him, we will know him, our neighbor, and ourselves within the fulfillment of his purpose of redeeming love. To learn to live in love with God and neighbor, this is the constraint that draws us together, holds us together in study and reflection, and sends us forth as ambassadors of the Christ.

Our love, indeed, is a response to his love. But Jesus reminds us in our lesson that God wants us to share the fellowship that is marked out by God's love of us. God yearns for our love toward him and the neighbor. When we love him with our whole being, and when we love the neighbor as one who shares with us creaturely, needy humanity, we truly enter the fellowship marked by Christ. We are here together to understand more clearly what it means to love God and man.

At the heart of Christian faith is the conviction that God's gift of the mind is not truly understood as his gift until it is given in service to him: "Thou shalt love the Lord thy God with all thy heart, and soul, and mind."[4] We give our thought to God, put to the service of love. We will love him with our minds. Our thought will be directed toward him and not away from him. We will love him with thought that never comprehends him fully, but finds fulfillment in placing the mind upon the altar of God. The mind joins the emotions and will in consecration to living out the love of God to God and neighbor. Love that is bereft of the mind of man is not a complete love. The love of God requires all there is of a man to love: "Thou shalt love the Lord thy God with all thy heart, and soul, and mind."[5]

We are here to grow together in the understanding of love. As the intellectual center of the church's life, the seminary offers to the most high God the tokens of minds that love him and reflect upon his revelation to his glory and to the service of men. The emotion that rejoices, the will that acts, and the mind that reflects—all of these are the marks of love. It is our special responsibility to stimulate the mind, knowing that such service is the mark of love.

Let us beware lest we substitute knowledge of the mind for the knowledge of the whole man. Let us caution ourselves to remember that knowledge *about* God is not the same as knowledge *of* God. Let us remember that understanding written on the pages of a book must be written on the tablets of the heart. Let us covenant that no idols of the mind will bar our access to the altar of God. Let us give up our minds to God to be taught by him out of the treasures of his grace. And let us never suppose that we love God more by sacrificing the mind than we do by using it.

There are some ministers of his word, I am sad to say, who live in the fear that the mind, the gift of God, if exercised, will not take them to God, but will take God from them. So, they warm up the heart and freeze the mind. And they put a halo around their mischief and call it the gospel. Let us dedicate our minds to God. Let us probe every path that offers a prospect. Let us think every thought that gives a clue. Let us offer our thought in love and pray God to cleanse us of all that distorts the revelation and darkens the vision of his love.

The mind that gives itself with heart and deed in love of God and neighbor will not be disappointed. The knowledge granted the mind will be the reality of the God and Father of our Lord and Savior Jesus Christ. In love we give our minds to the service of love. And in finding the meaning of love, we will find the meaning of life God has revealed to us. Our mind will be gathered up to his mind. And we will understand the meaning of his truth. Dante closed his *Divine Comedy* with these words:

> O grace abounding, whence I daring won
> > To fix my gaze upon the Eternal Light
> > So long that I consumed my sight thereon!
>
> I saw within its depths how it receives,
> > By love together in one volume bound,
> > What through the universe is scattered leaves.[6]

Only the mind, soul, and heart given to Christ can grasp the reality that it is the austere and tender hand of God which gives wholeness and integrity to his created order.

O Lord of all wisdom, thrust us forth today into an

unending devotion to thy truth revealed in Christ. Save us today from contentment with small thoughts that cost us nothing and give us no reward. Stir within us a passion for thought that costs us everything and gives us all that is needful. Teach us the thrill of living in devotion to thy truth revealed in Christ. Help us to know what is worth knowing, to love what is worth loving, and to praise what alone gives joy and gladness. Grant us loving understanding and understanding love, known only by those whose life is lived in the life of Christ, in whose name we pray. Amen.

10
The Fire on the Altar

Let us all pray silently to God and let us praise God, Lord of heaven and earth. Let us confess our sin and our sins. Let us give thanks to God for his love, for his forgiveness, for his peace, for hope born of the risen Christ. Let us give thanks to God for the good gifts of everyday life, for families that love and sustain us, for friends who understand us, for churches that trust us, for the call of God that does not forsake us. Let us pray for others, for all men over all the earth, for all who hate us, for all who love us, for all who misunderstand us, for all who believe in us. We bring our prayers to thee, O Lord, in the name of our Lord Jesus. Amen.

Every man of faith has two altars in his life: the altar in the church and the altar in the heart. The altar in the church is suggested for us in the word of the sixth chapter of Leviticus in the words, "Fire shall be kept burning on the altar; it shall never go out."[1] And the altar of the heart is suggested by the words found in 2 Timothy, chapter 1, "Stir into flame the gift . . . which is within you."[2] There is a fire in the midst of the people of God, and there is the fire in the recesses of the heart. All of it is the fire of God. And the care of the fire on the altar is the stewardship of the man of God.

A chapel meditation presented on October 9, 1968.

It is no accident that God has placed an altar among his people. And it is no mistake to speak of a smoldering fire in the heart that must be swept into flame. The altar reminds us of God's claim upon his people, and the fire reminds us of God's power within our hearts.

From the most ancient times, among various people, fire has been a significant feature of mythology, poetry, and cosmology. In the tales of ancient Greece, Prometheus lighted a torch in the chariot of the sun and gave the gift of fire to men. In the civic devotions of Rome, the vestal virgins tended the fire on the sacred altar, so that it never went out. Among the ancient Jews, there was a tradition that God himself had kindled the flame upon his altar when the Temple was built. He was the God who in the distant days of pilgrimage had looked down upon the pilgrims' journey by night in a pillar of fire to give them light (Ex. 13:21). God had lighted the fire on the altar, but he had left his word to men, "The fire shall be kept burning on the altar; it shall never go out." The flame would glow from the service of men who loved him.

There is a fire that burns in the church, and men of faith keep it kindled. It shall not go out. Fire on the altar of the church is *ours* to kindle; fire on the altar of the heart is *ours* to fan into flame.

The fire on the altar of the ancient Temple of Israel was a reminder that God was Lord of his people. A community of faith was the recipient of God's fiery reminder that he was the Lord. The fire on the altar was set in the midst of the people of God. Not solitary men of faith, but people in a community of faith are the recipients of the gift of the fire.

Sacrifices of bulls and goats on man-made altars no longer mark our faith. But the perpetual fire on the altar remains a beautiful symbol of the abiding presence of God among his people. More than twenty years ago, I went with a group of eleven- and twelve-year-old boys to a synagogue in New Haven, Connecticut. The youngsters saw a tiny light that burned and asked what it was. "It is the eternal light," the rabbi replied. "It never goes out." "But," said one little boy, "what happens to it when all the lights go out?" There is no light that shines upon our chapel day and night but the light of God's presence. And there is no perpetual light here except the light of kindling devotion born from a sense of the presence of God. Our devotion is placed upon his altar and his presence fans it into flame.

> Thou my best thought, by day or by night,
> Waking or sleeping, thy presence my light.[3]

Gathering here, we tend the fire upon the altar. We remember the God who tabernacles among his people, a God who refines and purifies and inspires.

The fire on the altar reminds us also of God's ceaseless care. He cares enough for us to remind us of his care. For we gather, as men did in yesteryear, at the altar of God. And the sacrifices we offer are the best gifts we have to offer— lives that love and hate, that believe and doubt, that keep faith and betray, that hope and despair. But God cares enough for us to ask us to come to his altar.

> Joy of the desolate, light of the straying,
> Hope of the penitent, fadeless and pure!
> Here speaks the Comforter, tenderly saying,
> "Earth has no sorrow that heav'n cannot cure."[4]

The fire on the altar teaches us yet something else. It is a reminder of our ceaseless praise. God lights the fire, but man puts the wood on the altar. God could easily tend the fire on the altar of the church, but that is not his way with men. He wants *us* to tend the fire. He wants *us* to come to him, to remember him, to show our awareness of him, to praise him. He has come to us to teach us to come to him. Long ago, Augustine said, "Without God we cannot, and without us God will not." He wants our loyalty and our praise. And the house of God is a reminder that his will is that we praise him and thank him.

One day, years ago, in New England, when the Puritans had gathered for worship, the earth became suddenly and terribly dark. Great fear came upon many of the worshipers (so sudden and complete was the darkness), and some insisted that the Day of the Lord had come. One elder arose in the church and cried, "Let the candles be lighted!" There was a man who knew that life is a vestibule to the temple of God's presence. And preparation for the service of the unending praise of God in the life to come begins in the life that has already come.

The fire on the altar reminds us also of God's call to devotion. God cares when we care and when we do not care. And we care because God cares. We say of someone that he is a devoted father, perhaps, or that he is a devoted son. And this is a great word to say of someone whom we know. The fire on the altar of God must be kindled by the devotion of men. We must tend the fire. Have we tended the fire on the altar?

In Eugene O'Neill's drama *Long Day's Journey Into Night,* one character says of the woman whose life is steadily deteriorating, "She hasn't denied her faith, but she's forgotten it, until now there's no strength of the spirit left in her."[5] Have we forgotten our faith? Have we brought the sacrifices of loving, if wayward, hearts to him to brighten our lives and the lives of others? "The fire shall be kept burning on the altar; it shall never go out."

> Breathe on me, Breath of God,
> Till I am wholly thine,
> Till all this earthly part of me
> Glows with thy fire divine.[6]

We come here today, men and women whom God has called to attend his altar. How well we know the vanity of an empty form and of an empty word. And it seems to us, at times, that the fire has gone out in church. It has not burned up; it has burned out. And the coals seem ashen gray. And to blow on them scatters ashes to the winds. And yet in the recesses of the soul, we have been apprehended by the reality that teaches us, as Studdert-Kennedy once said, that communion with God is not a luxury, but a necessity for the soul.

There is a word for us in 2 Timothy: "Stir into flame the gift . . . which is within you." There is an altar in the heart. And the fire has been placed upon it by the Lord who put fire upon the altar of his Temple. "Stir into flame the gift . . . which is within you." Perhaps in tending the fire at the altar in church, the fire in the heart will kindle into flame. We are those, Paul writes to Timothy, whose call is from God, whose mandate is divine, and whose power is the gospel. We may be weary in his work; but let us never grow weary of it. "Stir into flame the gift . . . which is within you."

Let us gather in this place, day by day, tapers and torches lighted by God's power on the altars of our hearts, and the fire on the altar in God's house will never go out.

> O Thou who camest from above,
> The pure celestial fire t'impart,

Kindle a flame of sacred love
On the mean altar of my heart.

There let it for thy glory burn
With inextinguishable blaze,
And trembling to its source return
In humble prayer and fervent praise.[7]

Let us pray.

God of our fathers, who brightens us with thy light, make warm our devotion to thee, that we may be worthy of our name. We pray through Christ our Lord. Amen.

11
The Hidden
and Revealed God

Father in heaven, we turn to thee because thou art worthy of all praise. Thou hast created us. Thou hast sustained us. Thou wilt call us to glory. We rejoice in the God of Abraham, Isaac, and Jacob, and the God and Father of our Lord and Savior, Jesus Christ.

We confess in penitence, O Lord, that we have sinned against thee and thy law. Forgive us. Calling ourselves men of faith, we confess that often anxiety rules us. Remembering the law of love, we know that hostility is often the gall of our hearts. Claiming the hope that is born of the risen Lord, we yet make despair the rule of life. O thou whose unwearying mercy is our salvation, have mercy upon us.

We remember with joy the unbounded gifts of divine grace. For families that gladden our heart, for friends who share our calling, for work that is devout, for a mission rooted in thy heart and growing in ours, we bless thee, O Lord, and will bless thee all the days of this life.

We pray, our Father, for all who gather here today, and for all men, whether they confess thy name or reject thee. Whatever we gain, O Lord, in this life, may we never lose thee. Whatever we lose, O Lord, may we win thee. Fan into flame the flickering tapers of our devotion, that we may burn with the light touched by the light of the world, who shines in our darkness.

A chapel meditation presented on January 30, 1969.

Gather us into thy strong arms, wide enough to gather us and all men into thy redeeming purpose. Through Christ our Lord. Amen.

Verily thou art a God that hidest thyself, O God of Israel, the Saviour.
(Isaiah 45:15, King James Version)

"Between God and us there stands the hiddenness of God."[1] This quotation, taken from the *Dogmatics* of Karl Barth, is, I think, the truth. And when pondering this meditation for today, it occurred to me that I ought to read in the *Dogmatics* and learn what Barth meant by that statement. But then I decided I did not want to know that much about it!

"Between God and us there stands the hiddenness of God." Let the theologian—and I use this term generously and in a pedestrian sense, to refer to you and to me— ponder this word of Barth. The theologian would much more likely say, "Between God and us there stands the revelation of God." And to say this would be to tell the truth. It would make the theologian happy. But there is another true word which may not put the theologian so much at ease, namely, "Between God and us there stands the hiddenness of God."

The ancient prophet of Israel once declared, "Verily thou art a God that hidest thyself, O God of Israel, the Saviour."[2] The prophet proclaims that God not only reveals himself, he hides himself. The context of the prophetic word leaves us free to ponder in the light of our faith what the prophet meant to convey to us. How is it that devout men can declare that God hides himself, and yet call that affirmation "faith"? Does the prophet say that because he doubts? No!

The context of the word suggests that he simply tells the truth. God does hide himself. And it is not faith to deny it. It is faith to declare it—"Verily thou art a God that hidest thyself."

What does the word of Isaiah mean to us today? It means, first of all, that the hidden God is the revealed God. God is not discovered but revealed. The prophetic word means that men may undertake to look for God in an effort to assure themselves of their genius. Well, in a case like that, God is not beyond a little holy "hide-and-seek." Man simply is never able to say, "I have found him! In my native genius, at the end of my brilliant search, I have found him!" Isaiah was saying you do not find God at the end of a long trail. In the most unexpected ways and times, *he* finds *you*.

Isn't this something we have learned in our most holy faith? He is hidden and revealed to faith in a baby in a manger. He is hidden and revealed to faith in a man crucified between malefactors. He is hidden and revealed to faith in a man raised from the dead. Revelation is there—a revelation of God himself. But it is hidden where human wisdom would never find it and where faith, the gift of God, *always does*! God's greatest revelations are hidden away from all human wisdom and revealed only to humble trust. Paul wrote to the church at Corinth, "What no one ever saw or heard,/What no one ever thought could happen,/Is the very thing God prepared for those who love him."[3]

The hidden God is revealed only to faith. And where there is no faith, the revealed God is hidden. Jesus said, "I thank thee, Father, Lord of heaven and earth, that thou hast hidden these things from the wise and understanding and revealed them to babes."[4]

What does the word of Isaiah mean to us today? It means, in the second place, that the revealed God remains the hidden God. And this fact is not one the theologian easily accepts. After all, is it not the duty of the expert to reveal his subject? What expert is prepared to glory, not in what he knows, but in what he does not know? The theologian is prepared to accept the observation that the hidden God is revealed, but is he prepared to accept the observation that the revealed God is hidden?

It is one of our great temptations that we want to live by faith *and* sight. How good to bolster faith with knowledge that makes faith less demanding and less all-encompassing. One of the cleverest ways to do this (and it seems exceptionally pious) is to bolster faith by ferreting out holy secrets through the wizardry of esoteric excavations of biblical texts. If we can remove more and more veils from God, if we can point to proof that proves faith, how in heaven's name could we otherwise have it so good? One of the cleverest sins of the theologian is to try to take the wraps off God in the name of faith.

But the revealed God remains the hidden God. God does not deliver himself into human hands, not even into the holy hands of theologians. Karl Barth has reminded us that God is not an object we can subjugate to our spiritual supervision and control. It is not our business to bolster faltering faith by mastering God. It is not our business to take faith out of faith. It is our business to live by faith and not by sight. Whenever we require God to submit to us, he hides from us and waits until we submit ourselves to him. I am deeply troubled by the kind of Christianity that assures man that if he gets the right key, he will be able to take the mystery out of God. I am wary of a Christianity that takes the faith out of faith.

Does this mean that faith will not express itself through theology? No, indeed! But it does mean that theology will always be the servant of faith, not its master. Martin Luther once said that God is held not in the hand but in the heart.

We who officiate at the altar must be content with the revelation that is granted. Nothing of God remains hidden from us which faith cannot trust to God. Faith can trust the hiddenness of God, because of the revelation of God in his Son, our Lord. Faith can live without answers because it lives with assurance that is the gift of the Holy Spirit.

John once wrote, "Beloved, we are God's children now; it does not yet appear what we shall be, but we know that when he appears we shall be like him, for we shall see him as he is."[5] That is faith. The God who is hidden has been revealed. And the God who has been revealed remains hidden. And faith, which accepts what has been revealed, trusts God with what is hidden. That is faith. And faith is the life of the theologian. Faith remembers with Isaiah the prophet that the God who is hidden is the Savior of Israel. Let us pray.

Father in heaven, who in grace takes our words to proclaim thine, redeem our words that we may be drawn to him who is higher than the highest heaven and nearer than the beating of our own hearts. Through Christ our Lord. Amen.

12
Free in Christ

*Almighty God our Father, this is the day thou hast made.
And we rejoice and are glad in it. We thank thee that as we
come to thee, we are conscious that thou hast long since
come to us. We rejoice in the great gift of our salvation and
for the life that is ours in thine only Son. Give us so to know
Christ in his life that the same mind which was in him may
be in us, that we may be in the world as he was in the
world. Give us so to know Christ in his death that we may
not glory, save in his cross whereby the world is crucified
unto us and we unto the world. Give us so to know Christ
in the power of his resurrection that like as he was raised
from the dead by the glory of the Father, we also may walk
in newness of life. In the name of Jesus Christ our Lord.
Amen.*

> **Freedom is what we have—Christ has set us free!
> Stand, then, as free people, and do not allow your-
> selves to become slaves again.**
> **(Galatians 5:1, Today's English Version)**

There is no more fitting word with which to begin a new
term than this one: "Freedom is ours! Christ has set us
free!" It is very easy in a setting like ours to become petty
slaves because we allow ourselves to be seduced by little

A chapel meditation presented on September 19, 1969.

things. And there is the slavery that is always the temptation of the person who wants to be good, the temptation to save oneself. So this text greets us as we begin a new term: "Freedom is what we have—Christ has set us free! Stand, then, as free people, and do not allow yourselves to become slaves again."[1]

"Freedom is what we have," Paul declares. Emancipation from the tyranny of law, sin, and death, this is what we have. The chains of self-propelled salvation, of violation of the will of God, of spiritual isolation from God the Father, these have dropped from us, and we live as the free children of God. We possess the experience of living as free men. There is in us the reality of forgiveness of sin and the assurance of sonship. There is an emancipation from the powers and the principalities, seen and unseen, that would undo us. We possess the reality that belongs only to those who are the children of God, gathered in Jesus Christ. We know the glorious freedom of the children of God.

Freedom of the gospel is not something we talk about only. We possess it. Or, it possesses us. We have freedom because we have faith. Because we live by faith, we live in freedom. "Freedom is what we have—Christ has set us free!" Our freedom is the gift of grace. Something has been born to us that never could have been born of us. There has been done for us what we could never have done for ourselves.

It is a part of our nature, however, to be confident of our mastery of everything we want to master. So we indulge on the one hand, and deny ourselves on the other, always reserving the intention of making things right in time. But when that moment of reckoning arrives, freedom does not come. It never comes if we must bring it. It comes as God's gift. So we rejoice that we have been given something very dear, freedom, the freedom to be truly God's intended men and women, the freedom to be the children of God.

There is something in us that makes it difficult for us to admit that it takes God to save us. We are not happy admitting that we cannot save, that we are only good at getting lost. There is something in us that makes us want to be free of God, and to call that "freedom." It is a part of God's gift to teach us that the freedom he gives us is the freedom to confess our sins and to find freedom in bondage to his will. So we are most truly free when we are most fully bound to the source and norm and goal of our freedom.

> He breaks the pow'r of canceled sin,
> He sets the pris'ner free. [2]

Our freedom is not found in independence from God, but in dependence upon him.

"Stand, then, as free people." Freedom is a way of living. We show our freedom by living it. We are free when we live out a life of faith. We are free when we act in freedom. Being Christian is being free. Our freedom is the obedience of faith.

Paul knew very well that it is difficult for us to stand as free people. It is a temptation of good people to suppose that perhaps they can stand as free persons a little better if they shore up their faith with some self-help. But freedom is not found in man-made or man-controlled security. We cannot escape from the freedom of faith to the security of self-imposed assurance. The temptation of the good person is to help God out. And the good person, who is also a theologian (and some good people are theologians) certainly does not want to strain God's grace by basking in it with abandon. So he decides not to glory in prodigal grace (fearful that that will be too much, even for God) but in a prim and proper grace that does not overdo this free gift of God.

And, lo and behold, so often a prim and proper grace issues in little faith. The God of a prim and proper grace is served by little faith. But, you see, where there is little faith, there is pygmy freedom. The person who possesses little faith never says, "Freedom is what we have—Christ has set us free! Stand, then, as free people."

The person with little faith is not a free person, but a frightened one. And such a person is most frightened by the bigness of salvation. Some persons' freedom is prison, because it opens no windows, walks through no doors, and never looks up to the blue sky. But our freedom is not imprisonment in creaky creeds or petty dogmas or pious piffle. And faith is not circumscribed by these, but it is emancipated from them. The free person trusts himself utterly to God's grace through faith. He knows that a turning to self is a turning from faith. And to turn from faith is to exchange freedom for slavery. Slavery comes from not trusting faith.

Our freedom in Christ involves not only our casting away self-help and a limiting faith. It means commitment. Paul the apostle teaches us that we trust ourselves truly to God when we accept as a trust the awareness that in some measure God has trusted others to us. We commit ourselves to God as we commit ourselves to the neighbor. When Paul writes to the Corinthians, he reminds them that freedom expresses itself fully not when it turns attention upon self, but when it abandons itself to others. We are truly free when we truly love. And when we love, we are free. Christian freedom is found not in isolation, but in community; not in nurture of self, but in nurture of others.

What does it mean to say, "Freedom is what we have—

Christ has set us free!"? It means to trust ourselves to God. It means to believe that faith and faith alone saves us. It means that we will not fabricate little theologies that fence in minitruths and label them "whole gospel." It means that we will live by faith, and not theology. You cannot be saved by theology.

To be free is to belong to Christ. It is to bring him our hopes, our joys, our fears, our failures, our doubts, our wanderings, our limitations at the beginning of this term. And it is to say to him,

> Make me a captive, Lord,
> And then I shall be free;
> Force me to render up my sword,
> And I shall conqueror be.
>
> I sink in life's alarms
> When by myself I stand;
> Imprison me within Thine arms,
> And strong shall be my hand.[3]

13
Treasure
in Earthen Vessels

For it is the God who said, "Let light shine out of
darkness," who has shone in our hearts to give the
light of the knowledge of the glory of God in the face
of Christ. But we have this treasure in earthen
vessels, to show that the transcendent power belongs
to God and not to us. We are afflicted in every way,
but not crushed; perplexed, but not driven to
despair; persecuted, but not forsaken; struck down,
but not destroyed; always carrying in the body the
death of Jesus, so that the life of Jesus may also be
manifested in our bodies. For while we live we are
always being given up to death for Jesus' sake, so that
the life of Jesus may be manifested in our mortal
flesh. So death is at work in us, but life in you. . . . So
we do not lose heart. Though our outer nature is
wasting away, our inner nature is being renewed
every day. For this slight momentary affliction is
preparing us for an eternal weight of glory beyond all
comparison, because we look not to the things that
are seen but to the things that are unseen; for the
things that are seen are transient, but the things that
are unseen are eternal.
(2 Corinthians 4:6-12,16-18)

The other night when my wife came home from church, I

A chapel meditation presented on January 29, 1970.

was toiling away on what I would say today. She asked me what it was I intended to speak about, and she said, "Well, you've talked about that before. I was there when you spoke on that text." And I said, "Well, what did I say?" "Well," she said, "I don't know." That gave me considerable relief, and then I began to think. I said, "Yes, I think I have spoken on that text. And as I remember, John Eddins was present in the summer school chapel the day I preached on that text. I think maybe I had better call him and find out what I said." But instantly I thought better of it. And I said to myself, "No, a professor does well to remember his own thoughts. He certainly cannot be expected to remember the thoughts of others." So, taking renewed heart, I say with the words of Paul in another context, "This is the third time I am coming to you."

Now this word of Paul that we have read reminds us of our Christian existence. We have a treasure. And the apostle is specific about what this treasure is. It is the light of the revelation of the glory of God in the face of Jesus Christ. It is the good news that God loves sinners. It is the proclamation that God acts to bring man into his loving purpose through the life, death, and resurrection of Jesus Christ. It is the glorious treasure of redemption. And it is not so much that we have the treasure as it is that the treasure has us! The treasure is the gospel, and the gospel is God at work in Jesus Christ. The treasure is the word of God at work in us.

But this treasure that we possess never leads us to arrogant boasting or to spurious self-assurance. This precious prize that transforms our human existence into Christian existence is God's gift and not man's work. So then, our Christian existence tells us something about ourselves that has been made possible by the treasure of the gospel of Christ.

Further, the word of the apostle makes us aware of our mortality. It does this, first of all, by reminding us that faith does not preserve us from the hard realities of human existence. Christian existence is not the absence of human existence, but human existence transformed. God does not write into any confession of faith a favored person's clause that exempts the faithful from the tribulations of this life. Not in the absence of life's hard realities, but in their presence, the Christian disciple finds the thread of Christian purpose, however tangled or knotted at times it may seem to be. Paul speaks plainly of the darkness and the brightness of Christian existence, "We are often troubled, but not crushed; sometimes in doubt, but never in despair. There are many enemies; but, we are never without a friend. And though badly hurt at times, we are not destroyed."[1]

Now clearly in this context he means to emphasize to us the resources that we have in this life; nevertheless, he makes clear that there is the darkness as well as the brightness in the Christian life. And it comes, this darkness does, to the Christian as well as to the non-Christian in the world. Life has its way of reminding us that we Christians, too, are earthen vessels. *We* are scarred; *we* are marred; *we* are shattered; *we* are broken—just like other men. Our salvation does not lie in our indestructibility, but in the power of God who makes all things new.

But a second remarkable thing about the Christian understanding of life is that recognition of human limitation does not qualify life but emancipates it. It does not cripple it; it heals it. It does not ground it; it gives it wings. In understanding our mortality, our humanity, we learn to trust God. "We have this treasure in earthen vessels, to show that the transcendent power belongs to God and not to us." We understand our limitation as God's possibility.

We see our frailty as God's strength. Our mortality becomes the instrument of his immortality.

This word of Paul also authenticates our mission. We live life in terms of the cross: self-denying, self-emptying, forgiving, serving, loving. In the very same experiences that try the souls of all men, the disciple of Christ lives out the meaning of life he has learned from Christ. Not only is the Christian not exempt from the trials of life, he is called to live a redeemed life that becomes a redeeming life, because it becomes a means by which God tells again the story of the sacrificial love of his Son. The Christian is called to die for the Lord who died for him. And he dies by living the dying of Jesus. Our dying takes place by living for him in terms of the cross, so that the Christian does not wear out, he lives out.

So the God who works in us works through us. At the very times when life is hard for us, Christ is at work in us. Jesus is visible in our lives when no victory within our lives is visible to us. Those who see his cross at work in us will sense his resurrection in us. But men do not know the resurrection in us until they have seen the cross in us. Life comes through death still! To the Philippians, Paul wrote that all he wanted was "that I may know him and the power of his resurrection, and may share his sufferings, becoming like him in his death, that if possible I may attain the resurrection from the dead."[2]

This word of the apostle, last of all, reminds us that our resources are invisible. We do not turn back in pilgrimage if we do not stand vindicated before the eyes of men. When we look back we see the crucified one and the light of the knowledge of God's glory shining in his face. And we look up! And in the words of the apostle in the eighteenth verse of this chapter, "we look not to the things that are seen but to the things that are unseen." In trust in Christ, in faith, we nurture our lives, so that in spending our lives for Christ, we do not spend ourselves but find the renewal he gives unto the perfect day. Faith does not count the success or the failure but the fidelity. Faith does not become disconsolate in the midst of this life because its eyes are set upon the unseen that is veiled by a heavenly Father who will not disappoint our faith in his Son. We need no outward sign of victory, because we are kept by the victory of the cross which is planted in the castles of our hearts.

Let us begin the new term by remembering the high calling that is ours in our most holy faith: to live to die, and to die to live.

Holy Father, take our words and use them in thy word in the world thou dost love. Through Christ our Lord. Amen.

14
Heralds
of Good Tidings

Almighty God our Father, we rejoice that thou dost receive us gladly when we confess our sins. And we pray thee now to renew our souls as we live this day. Receive our thanks for every token of thy grace and every mark of thy bounty and teach us to rest ourselves in thee. Make thyself known to us today as thou art in Christ, that we may be the instruments of thy will as thou doest thy great work in the world. Through Christ our Lord. Amen.

Then they said one to another, we do not well: this day is a day of good tidings, and we hold our peace.
(2 Kings 7:9, King James Version)

Our text for today, 2 Kings 7:9, tells of a time that tried men's souls. Some of God's people were in the stress of hard times, literally starving to death, surrounded by an enemy that simply kept waiting until they were helpless. A small band of lepers lived just outside the city walls. Life was exceptionally hard for them. They were cut off from all sides, and famine was rampant. They faced certain death. What could they do? Well, they became heroes! Those four lepers set forth the evangelical word of our text, "This day is a day of good tidings."[1] How in the world did they get the

A chapel meditation presented on September 17, 1970.

83

consent of their minds and lips for a testimony like that?

First of all, they faced reality. They did not bewail their lot. They did not berate the people who placed them outside the walls. They did not form a committee—a clear indication that they were neither Baptists by lineage nor professors by vocation. They did not call a prayer meeting but a brainstorming session. As a matter of fact, they had a little existential group therapy. They arrived at three alternative courses of action, all three of which ended with the same possibility, death. They faced reality with all its grim possibilities. When they had finished their musings, they went out to face the worst the camp of the enemy could offer. And that was the first step they took on the road to hero-hood: they faced reality.

Those of us who are the servants of God today at times are like those four lepers. We often feel cut off from the sacred precincts of many well-meaning people of small faith who are walled in, under spiritual attack (often times they do not know it!), and slowly starving, with very little deep spiritual understanding. But this is no time to bewail our lot. Nor is it a time to remind God of how sad it is to be his servants. Rather, we face reality. And there must not be left any unprobed sacred precincts of reality for perceptive ministers of Jesus Christ. We understand our situation both in reference to the walled-in city, and the world of the Syrians. Those of us who are here today are gathered in this theological community to face the unmasked visage of reality. We employ every gift of learning and examine any point of view in an effort to discern just what truth is. Made free in Christ, we are free to face truth, wherever it leads us. We have not gathered here to avoid reality, but to probe it. And this for us, as well as for the lepers, may be the beginning of our redemption.

We learn also from our lesson that this tiny band found

salvation where they feared destruction. They found life where they would not have been surprised to find death. They went into the camp of the enemy and found that he had fled.

What if they had spent their time outstripping one another in painting pictures of the awesome strength of those who would overcome them? What if they had dwelt upon their feeble strength compared with the might of so many? With good reason they could have slipped back into the city and died slowly with everybody else. But no! They decided to live in the world where the Syrians were. At least, and at worst, death there would come at the end of high adventure! They took a chance on being able to stay alive in a world that was not walled in. And as a result, they found salvation where they feared destruction.

It is a big world, this school is, in a little place. There are no walls here to protect our theological insecurities. There is only a bigger world than many of us have ever lived in before. And we can either live in it or die in it. Now here is an opportunity for salvation. Accept it, and opportunity becomes possession.

When I began teaching eighteen years ago, I had in one of my classes a small group of men who listened very carefully to what I said. But some of them never said anything to expand what I said; they always made statements that contracted it. So fearful were they that they would lose Christ, they never really ventured to find him. Afraid he would become smaller, they never learned how big he really is!

There is a big world beyond the walls of this campus, and we live in it as committed men and women. And we find life there, not death. There are not only Syrians there. There is also God.

Last of all, these heroes in our text became heralds of a

new world. If they had remained in the shadow of the wall, or if they had retired within the gates of the city, they would never have seen God do some of his work. They suddenly found themselves surrounded by the treasures of a new world. Their first reaction was to revel in what was now theirs. But then they had another council. The upshot of it all was that they decided not to hide it or to preserve it, but to share it. They said, "We do not well: this day is a day of good tidings, and we hold our peace."

They ran to tell others what they had found. Hal Luccock once said, "Good news cannot walk. It runs."[2] Some of you who are here know that one of my best little friends is David Shriver, the son of Dr. George Shriver, who teaches church history. Now and again, when I see David on the campus, we go together to get ice cream at the campus store. And I remember a year ago when I saw David on the campus, I said, "David, let's go get some ice cream." His face lighted up, and he said, "Let me go get my sisters!' Now David was acting like a good theologian. When Jesus was raised from the dead, the women ran to tell the disciples. Little David had good news he wanted to share with those sisters whom he loved very much. Those women had news to tell those who loved Jesus very much. "How beautiful upon the mountains are the feet of him that bringeth good tidings, that publisheth peace."[3]

Four souls had the message to ease anguish of the mind, to plant laughter in the eye and to renew strength of body and soul. To have been silent would have been to court disaster. There was a story that had to be told. They had to tell of the opportunities that were theirs outside the walls: "Come, see what God has done, not inside the walls but outside them."[4]

My brothers and sisters in Christ, we have good tidings to tell all the world. "I bring you good tidings of great joy,"[5] the angel said one night to a shepherd band. Christians are a blissful and joyous people. This is still our Father's world, and he is at work in Christ. We cannot hold our peace or the stones will cry out. "Get you up to a high mountain,/O Zion, herald of good tidings;/lift up your voice with strength,/O Jerusalem, . . ./say to the cities of Judah,/ 'Behold your God!'"[6]

All men need to see what God has done and is doing for all his people. Everywhere there are footnotes in the long documentation of God's deeds in behalf of men. All of us who share in his work in Christ must share it with others.

The claim upon our devotion is a claim this day pressed upon us: "We do not well: this day is a day of good tidings." We must not hold our peace.

We give thee our thanks, O Lord, for so great a redeemer, who calls us and has pointed out the way for us to travel. Grant that we will be inspired by him who has marked out the path, and who calls us at its end. For thy name's sake. Amen.

15
A Presence That Disturbs Me

Father in heaven, we know that thou dost long to sustain us. But we come to thee in prayer because in expressing our spirits to thee we know the strength of thy Spirit. Quicken us this day to love and serve thee. Through Christ our Lord. Amen.

"I have felt/A presence that disturbs me with the joy/Of elevated thoughts."[1] I am unsure what Wordsworth meant by this beautiful sentence. I am inclined to believe that he was saying that he sensed the presence of the divine in the world around him. But when I first came upon it, it struck me as a powerful affirmation of Christian experience. Whatever it meant to Wordsworth, it reminds me of two great affirmations of the Christian life, a disturbing presence and the elevation of joy.

Now there is an absence that disturbs us. And we are realistic about this. And for some men, sadly, it seems to be an unending absence. For most of us here, I suspect that there are times when there is an absence for a season. And I think it is very good that in such times we remember that the reality of God does not depend solely upon our feelings or upon our experiences. He is revealed in his Son. He reveals himself to us still through the Holy Spirit. And he manifests himself in the lives of the faithful. And at times in

A chapel meditation presented on February 3, 1971.

our own lives we wait patiently for his presence, remembering that it is not so much that he is absent from our presence as it is that we are absent from his.

Now there is a presence that disturbs me. It destroys my tranquillity and composure. It has a negative influence upon some people. Its influence upon my life may be negative. And this, I think, is the way some people have always reacted to Jesus. He has been to them a presence that disturbs them, that destroys their tranquillity and their composure. And he becomes in their lives, essentially, a negative influence. I think, for instance, of Jesus' own lifetime, when he went to preach for the first time in the synagogue at Nazareth before the people who knew him. According to Luke, after he preached, the people there were filled with wrath. Churchgoing people were disturbed by him. He disturbed the saints. And we learn that at another time the religious experts (according to Mark's Gospel) rather early in Jesus' life were disturbed by him. They took counsel how to destroy him. Again, there was a community in which a mentally deranged man was restored. And when these people learned what it was that had happened, they invited Jesus out of town. And it is very touching to note that on one occasion a man who was mentally disturbed coming into the presence of Jesus, or finding himself in the presence of Jesus, did not want Jesus to undo or to disturb the distorted vision of reality with which he had learned to live.

Now Jesus was a disturbing presence because he required a new center of reference, a new orientation of thinking, and a new pattern of life. And the great danger even for us who are here this morning, is that Jesus will be a negative influence upon us, a presence that merely destroys our tranquillity and our composure. And it very well may be that in our ways which are very clever and subtle—

and the ways of the theologian are particularly adept at this point—we may try to turn him off, turn him around, or turn him away. We need to give attention to Wordsworth's line. Is there a presence that disturbs me, that merely destroys my tranquillity and composure, and becomes a negative influence upon my life?

Now there is a presence that disturbs me and shatters my outlook, alters my thinking, and transforms my life. And this living presence becomes not a negative, but a positive influence upon my life. I remember reading of the time when Archbishop William Temple met Reinhold Niebuhr for the first time, and the Archbishop is supposed to have said to Mr. Niebuhr, "At last I meet the disturber of my peace." And those of us who were in divinity school in those years will remember that Reinhold Niebuhr was indeed the disturber of the peace of many men. He disturbed the peace of many men in such fashion as to shatter their outlook, alter their thinking, and transform their life in the light of the gospel of Jesus Christ.

Now it is also true that if there were people whose tranquillity and composure were shattered by the Christ of the Gospels, there were also people in that ancient time whose lives were disturbed by his presence and were thereby transformed. For instance, we read in Mark's Gospel that many of the common people heard him gladly. We remember that a leader like Nicodemus was deeply touched by him. And Levi the tax collector followed him. And one day a leper came to Jesus and said, "If you want to, you can make me clean." And all the Christian church, at its best, is testimony to us that this living presence can shatter our outlook, alter our thinking, and transform our life so that all of our life is an effort to reach up to him, to live with him, to transform our lives by his. There is a presence that disturbs me and transforms my life. "I have felt/A presence that disturbs me with the joy/Of elevated thoughts."

The story in the Gospels which reminds me of something of the insight of this line from Wordsworth is a story taken from the twenty-fourth chapter of the Gospel of Luke. It is a resurrection story, an Easter story. We read that two of the disciples were talking about what had happened in Jerusalem. And we read in the text that they were looking sad. And then, Jesus happened by. And they entered into conversation with him, not really knowing him fully. And he walked with them and talked with them. And then, toward the end of the day, they invited him to remain with them. And he did. And they entered into yet deeper fellowship with Jesus. And they knew him as he was. And, then, as they reflected upon their experience, they said, "Did not our hearts burn within us while he talked to us on the road, while he opened to us the scriptures?"[2]

Now we are the disciples of the Lord in our time, and there are situations in which, too, we look very sad. And we live in times which make it very easy for us to be disconsolate in our soul. But we do well to remember this story of the disciples when they were sad, too. When he is a presence in our daily lives, we learn who he is. When we walk with him and when we eat with him, we learn who he is. "Behold, I stand at the door and knock;" says the Lord. "If any one hears my voice and opens the door, I will come in to him, and eat with him, and he with me."[3] And so our hearts will burn within us, as did the hearts of those disciples long ago.

Men who really know who Christ is, who have felt his presence, possess a sense of joy. The apostle Paul reminds us throughout his letter to the Philippians of the joy of the Christian experience. And it is a note throughout the Scriptures. Paul Tillich spoke of joy as the fulfillment in our inner being, with the dimension of the eternal. And where there is fulfillment there is joy; and where there is joy there is fulfillment. There is the fulfillment in our inner being with the dimension of the eternal. That is our joy.

In the ninth book of his *Confessions,* after he had recited the story of his conversion, Augustine spoke of the joy that had come to him in his newfound Christian experience. And he said so beautifully about God, that he is "sweeter than all pleasure, . . . brighter than all light, . . . higher than all honor."[4] And he spoke of the great note of the Christian joy that had come into his life just before he spoke so sorrowfully and tenderly of the loss of his mother.

C. S. Lewis in a remarkable book, *Surprised by Joy,* has pointed out that the state of elevation of mind that he so much wanted throughout deep moments of his life was not a state of mind that he could induce, but a product of self-forgetfulness.

So it is true that we do not possess the joy of the gospel so much as that it possesses us. It is not our creation, but God's gift. Our thanksgiving becomes the basis and then the expression of joy. And our joy comes when we come to that presence that transforms us. We walk the road with the living Christ. We sit at table with the risen Christ. And he grants us joy. Karl Barth has put it very beautifully:

> When a man, any one of us, . . . looks up to him, to Jesus Christ, a momentous change takes place in him. The greatest revolution is unimportant by comparison. The transformation cannot be overlooked. It is manifest, quite simply, in so much as he who looks up to him and believes in him . . . may become a child of God. It is an inward change, yet it cannot possibly remain hidden. As soon as it occurs, it presses forcefully for outward manifestation. A great and enduring light brightly dawns on such a person. This

light is reflected on his face, in his eyes, in his behaviour, in his words and deeds. Such a person experiences joy in the midst of his sorrows and sufferings, much as he still may sigh and grumble. Not a cheap and superficial joy that passes, but deep-seated, lasting joy. It transforms man in his sadness into a fundamentally joyful being. . . . Such light and joy and laughter are ours when we look up to him, to Jesus Christ. He is the one who makes us radiant. We ourselves cannot put on bright faces. But neither can we prevent them from shining. Looking up to him, our faces shine.[5]

"I have felt/A presence that disturbs me with the joy/Of elevated thoughts."

16
Running the Race
That Is Set Before Us

> Therefore, since we are surrounded by so great a
> cloud of witnesses, let us also lay aside every weight,
> and sin which clings so closely, and let us run with
> perseverance the race that is set before us, looking to
> Jesus the pioneer and perfecter of our faith, who for
> the joy that was set before him endured the cross,
> despising the shame, and is seated at the right hand
> of the throne of God.
> (Hebrews 12:1-2)

This year at Southeastern Baptist Theological Seminary,
by the mercies of God, we begin our third decade of
service to Christ. More than 2300 students have received
degrees or certificates from our school. And in some
genuine senses as we meet today, we are surrounded by our
own cloud of witnesses. Most of them are very much alive,
faithful servants of Jesus Christ as they do his work in the
world.

James Moffatt chose grandly when he made the title of
one of his books *The Thrill of Tradition*. I do not know how
long it takes for an inspiring past to become a tradition. But
I find a thrill in our twenty years of service to Christ.
Twenty years does not seem very long, especially to those
of us who will consider ourselves fortunate if we live twenty

A chapel meditation presented on September 15, 1971.

more. But already our seminary knows what it means to look back on some of our own heroes of faith. Not far from this chapel, in a peaceful part of God's good earth, their physical bodies rest from their labor. Their names are now called among the heroes of faith, witnesses whose lives still touch us in our own journey of faith.

As we gather in chapel today, we are surrounded, then, by a cloud of witnesses that was created by the devotion of our own colleagues and also by many fathers in the history of faith. And we rejoice in that truth, that our souls may be renewed at the beginning of a new school year.

In our text today, the author introduces us to a grand "Therefore." That is his way of saying, "Look back in order to look ahead." There is a profound sense in which the Bible is a book that looks back—back to the Exodus, back to Calvary. The Bible spends a lot of time looking back. But there is something about its looking back that some folk never quite understand. It looks back in order to go forward. There are some Christian folk who look back in order to go back, in order to stay back. And when that can be done in the name of orthodoxy, it gives an especially unctious and holy contentment.

But the author of Hebrews invites us to look back at the eleventh chapter of his letter, to remind us of the great fathers of faith, and to go forward because we have looked backward. In that great chapter we read of those whose names are inscribed in the Hall of Fame of Faith. We learn what it means to see with the eye of faith, to trust in God, by which invisible realities become real for men who do not confuse the city of man with the city of God, who never set their tent pegs in concrete but keep on trek, who see beyond the horizon scanned by man's eye to the rim of the city of God visible only to faith.

There is a big difference between looking back and

finding inspiration for the future and looking back and finding inspiration for the past. We need to remember this term what it means to take the "Therefore" in Hebrews 12:1 seriously. We look back in order to look ahead.

Looking back with the Bible always leads to looking around. There is a host of witnesses encircling us— Abraham, Moses, the prophets, those who labored in our own community. They all gather with us today, doing what good witnesses do. They say, "It's so! It's worth it! Go on!" They do not gather on the sidelines because they have fallen out or because they refuse to fall in, but because they have finished the race. They are the victors who have trusted the Great Victor. And they would make us victors, too.

A number of years ago I ran across a sermon by Ralph Sockman with the title "Our Contemporary Ancestors." I have no idea what Dr. Sockman said in the sermon, but I will not forget the title because men of faith still have, I think, at least two kinds of contemporary ancestors. One type always wants to go back to Egypt, where life is simple and orderly and peaceful and controlled. They want to take us back to yesterday and leave us there. The other kind wants us to look for a city whose builder and maker is God. They bring yesterday to us today to point us to tomorrow. May the good Lord deliver us from all the contemporary ancestors who long for the fleshpots of Egypt. But let them gather around Abraham, Moses, the prophets, Peter, James, and John—all those who bear witness that they have crossed the finish line of faith. Summoned to adventure and conflict, they have won the victory of faith. Victors, they inspire us to victory. Gathering around us, the witnesses of true faith tell us to put aside everything that is a deflector, to get a mind-set that offers no clinging place for sin, to run the race and hold out.

I can think of no quality more surely necessary in a budding theologian—or in a fading one, for that matter—than the determination to hold on. Returning to the heroic devotion of men of faith in the eleventh chapter, the author of Hebrews says that they all won their record for faith.

The witnesses who surround us today remind us that life is a hard race to run. And at the heart of genuine faith is the heart to see it through. Discipline in the life of the spirit is inevitable in the life of any person who takes seriously the call of Christ. I have often wondered how much God would have been able to reveal to Abraham if he had never left Ur. Suppose Abraham had said, "Lord, I don't like to travel, and we don't have a jet camel yet." What could God have done for the world through Abraham if he had stayed at home and drunk Chaldean tea at three and taken leisurely camel rides around the neighborhood at dusk? Abraham had to exchange his security for God's security. He had to trust God's promise more than his own possessions. He had to make a journey, a long, hard pilgrimage. Every one of us has to leave his Ur and make the long, exacting, rewarding pilgrimage with God.

We learn in our text today that we not only look back and look around. We also look forward. We are admonished to keep our eyes fixed on Jesus, the pioneer and perfection of faith. Races are not won by men looking at their feet. They are won by men who know what their goal is and who keep their eye on it. Jesus—he is the example of faith. He is the embodiment of faith. He is the inaugurator, the inspirer, the goal of faith. He is faith lived out in a human life. He is the supreme vindication of faith.

Races in the Christian life are lost when eyes are taken off Jesus. When we really see him, we know what it means for him to have carried the cross and for us to be carried by it. We learn what it meant for him to die on it, and for us to live it. Looking ahead we see him, who steadily endured the cross, and we stay in the race. I cannot explain it. But I can testify that when faith keeps its eyes fixed on Jesus, it never stops learning.

Suddenly we are all aware that witnesses to faith are cheering on witnesses to faith. And we know in our hearts the joy that possessed the Lord. Why is it we come here, all of us? We come to find strength in the company of faithful men and women who have preceded us and who accompany us, to run the race of life more surely to God's glory, to keep our focus upon Jesus who draws us into the future and welcomes every soul who finishes the race.

17
"Sir, We Want to See Jesus"

Father in Heaven, we come to thee because thou art the Lord and because we are thy children. We gather in thy presence in thy house to hear thy word. We pray thee to grant us to hear it, truly to receive it, and to do it. For Jesus' sake. Amen.

Some Greeks were among those who had gone to Jerusalem to worship during the festival. They went to Philip (he was from Bethsaida in Galilee) and said, "Sir, we want to see Jesus." Philip went and told Andrew, and the two of them went and told Jesus. Jesus answered them, "The hour has now come for the Son of Man to receive great glory. I am telling you the truth: a grain of wheat remains no more than a single grain unless it is dropped into the ground and dies. If it does die, then it produces many grains. Whoever loves his own life will lose it; whoever hates his own life in this world will keep it for life eternal. Whoever wants to serve me must follow me, so that my servant will be with me where I am. And my Father will honor anyone who serves me."

(John 12:20-26, Today's English Version)

The lesson this morning teaches us that there were those

A chapel meditation presented on September 5, 1973.

who wanted to meet Jesus. They were serious, conscientious, God-fearing people. And they wanted to get acquainted with Jesus. So we are reminded today that there are those around us who have heard something about Jesus and want to meet him. And that should be a great joy, especially to us who gather here this morning. People now, as then, hear about Jesus and want to meet him.

Notice that these inquiring souls came to those who knew Jesus. We do not know precisely why they came to Philip and Andrew. Perhaps they had a well-known relationship to Greeks. What matters is that men who wanted to see Jesus approached those who knew Jesus, because they had lived with him and really knew him.

So the text reminds us that there are many earnest people who want to talk about Jesus. They want to speak to us, to hear what we have to say, to learn what we have learned from Jesus. What a wonderful ministry when someone inquires about Jesus and addresses me, "Tell me what you know about him. I want to meet him." We do not know whether these particular people ever met Jesus face to face. But it is clear that the word of Jesus goes forth to all who make earnest inquiry about him. He hears their voices and answers them. And blessed are those who accept his call to them, "Follow me."

Sometimes, I fear, Jesus has to yell his call over our heads to those he invites to follow him. It should be the easiest thing in the world for an inquirer to get good directions to Jesus from a preacher or teacher. But, as a matter of fact, the preachers and teachers of Jesus' day had not really seen him. We read in the chapter immediately preceding our text that they were looking for him in order to arrest him.

One of the great concerns of my life has been that people will come asking me the way to Jesus and I will not point out the way. The temptation of some professors is to say, "Well, take this bibliography, dear brother. Jot down any questions you have as you read along, and come see me in a few weeks. I'll give you another bibliography, not so modest, when you show up again." Or, if the professor has ever had a class in counseling, he may say when someone asks him about Jesus, "Well, what do you think about him?" A thriving theology student did come to me one day when I taught at Southern Seminary in Louisville and asked if I would explain the doctrine of the Trinity to him. I thanked him for his excessive generosity in numbering me among the theologians and asked him how much time he had to hear my answer. He looked at his watch and said, "Oh, I can give you five minutes."

Now the temptation of some students, I am afraid, is to box Jesus into their corner and yell, "Here he is!" But in fact, they may have succeeded only in confining and restricting the real Jesus in a fashion that tends to rob him of his glorious lordship, of spiritual freedom that is always beckoning us to larger fellowship and to larger understanding.

As we begin this academic year, I hope we will remember as teachers that when inquirers ask us about Jesus, they are not prepared to accept a Jesus substitute, namely, us. They want to get from us to him. And as servants of the Lord, there is no greater reward than following toward him. It has been said that one of the greatest paintings is Matthias Grünewald's *Crucifixion,* in which the center of attention is fixed entirely on that ghastly figure on the cross, the suffering for a whole world painted into his body.

And I hope that as students—and all of us are students in the kingdom of God—we will not build up walls so high that revelation will have to make an end run to get around our theological defenses. The professor-student relationship reminds me, at times, of a ride on those high-powered speed cars I have seen at the county fairs. The professor locks the student in tightly, shaking the door a bit to be sure he will not fall out. The student grasps the sides of the vehicle so tightly that veins stand up an inch on his hands, his eyes as big as cantaloupes. Then off he soars, engines roaring, bells clanging. Over hill and dale. And after three years, he gets back, manages to tear himself away from the sides of his theological speed machine (his eyes now as big as watermelons), and shaking himself after he gets out, he exclaims, "Thank God I've got my feet on the ground again!"

Now if all of us—all of us—sit at the feet of Jesus, we will be able in our own experience to say to all who ask to see him, "Come. I have seen him. I will point the way."

The Greeks who came to meet Jesus did really meet him. But the Jesus they met was much greater than they had imagined. They expected to see a man from Galilee and saw, instead, the Savior of the world. They heard him speak of dying, of loving life and losing it, of hating life and keeping it, of service and commitment, of service and glory. That is precisely what we learn when we really see Jesus and when we point others to him. We really see Jesus when we see the man on the cross calling us to the cross. From the cross and to the cross he draws people of every race and nation.

And stripped of our petty piety (so often the sin of the theological right) and our arrogant wisdom (so often the sin of the theological left), we learn at his cross that there we really meet God and ourselves. Through God's wondrous grace, we see Jesus. And the cross becomes the foundation of life, the interpretation of life, the goal of life—my glory all the cross!

> I know not how that Calvary's cross
> A world from sin could free;
> I only know its matchless love
> Has brought God's love to me.[1]

When we really see Jesus at the cross, we discover that we see him through faith. He calls us, and we trust in God's work in him. Seeing him on the cross, we see God. And faith becomes a way of living. Dietrich Bonhoeffer said, "Faith is only real when there is obedience, . . . and faith only becomes faith in the act of obedience. . . . Only he who believes is obedient, and only he who is obedient believes."[2]

When we really see Jesus at the cross, we learn also that we see him in discipleship. Again, Bonhoeffer said that Christianity without discipleship is always Christianity without price. And Christianity without price is always Christianity without discipleship.[3]

When we really see Jesus at the cross, we learn also that we see him in service. We learn that life is no longer lived in the old, selfish way. Love is placed at the center of our will, and all our days are given to the claim of God's love upon us as we express it in our love of others.

When we really see Jesus on the cross, we become free for the first time, free to become the sons and daughters of God. And the more we are bound to him by the cross, the more we are set free. Thanks be to God, men still come looking for Jesus. Thank God they still ask you and me, "Have you seen him? Can you tell us where he is?" We point them to the man on the cross. And he will call them to faith, discipleship, and service. And he will promise them, as he has promised us, that all of us will be with him where he is, to behold his glory.

18
Dreamers of the Dream

Almighty God our Father, we come to thee, those who are redeemed in Christ Jesus, and we confess our sin. We pray thee to come to us in this time of worship and renew our spirit. May we open our hearts to thee because we know thou hast long since opened thy heart to us. Through Christ our Lord. Amen.

> **I will pour out my Spirit upon all flesh,**
> **. . . . .**
> **and your young men shall see visions,**
> **and your old men shall dream dreams.**
> **(Acts 2:17)**

A few years ago, I read a book by Stewart Holbrook, entitled *Dreamers of the American Dream.*[1] It is a delightful book, and in many ways, very inspiring. It reminds us that we had forebears in this country who were convinced that life could be very different for many people. They had a conviction that they were called to help to make it different. Not all of them were successful, by any means, in their dreams, but they dreamed. And it is a pride of our heritage, it is a part of their legacy, that at our finest in this country, we like to believe that we are dreamers, that we

A chapel meditation presented on January 29, 1974.

are visionaries, and that there is a beautiful life to which we want to be captive, of which we want to be a part.

In his book, Holbrook says three things about these American dreamers which I find very fascinating. At the time I first read them, I thought immediately of another book. It, too, tells about dreamers. It is the Book of Acts. It was written a long time ago. And I like very much to be aware of that book, because it is a part of my heritage, too. It tells about my forebears who were dreamers, how on the day of Pentecost something stupendous happened to them. And when the question was raised by some who were there, "What does this mean?" and some of them replied, "This means that some folk have got drunk early!" there was one man who said, "No. I will tell you what it means. It means that God's work with his people through the centuries, made clear to us in the great prophet Joel, has come to pass. He told about people having visions and dreaming dreams. Now it has all come true. What you see happening," he said, "is a dream come true."

Now Peter continued to talk about God's dealing with the Jewish people in his sermon. And at the very end of it, he said to all who heard him, "Now this dream is meant for you and for your children and for all who are far away."[2] That means that we can come to the chapel this morning and hear about a dream come true, that was meant not simply for our forefathers of yesteryear, but is meant for us. The dream is meant for you, and your children, and for all who are far away.

Now when we look at what Holbrook said about American dreamers and when we look at what the author of Acts tells us about Christian dreamers, we find, I think, a word from God for us today. I am very sure that as we begin a new semester, it is an easy thing for all of us—students, faculty, and administration—to ponder whether we are beginning almost worn-out or whether we are hoping that we can catch a vision and have a spurt of vitality. We are not always sure, are we?

I am very sure that all of us in the midst of our work, especially when it comes piling in upon us, wonder at times if we are in God's work or if we are just preparing for it. And I think that one of the reminders that we need to bring to ourselves is that we are in God's work, and we need God's word where we are.

A. E. Day, the great Methodist preacher, in the early years of his life had a grave illness. He was told that he would have to leave the eastern part of the United States. He would have to go to the far West. He then had a great spiritual experience, he said, because he opened his heart to God as he never had before. The result of that was that he did not go West at all. He remained in the East and has lived a very long life. And in his book on prayer, he says that what he learned was that he did not need a new place to live in the West, but a new experience of God in the East.[3] And I think that in moments like these at the beginning of a new term, we may wish we were somewhere else. But, we are here. And we need a new experience of God where we are.

The Book of Acts, this book of dreams, reminds us of the same thing that Stewart Holbrook says about American dreamers. We learn that dreamers begin with a different point of reference. Now, there was all kind of wonderment about what was happening at the Day of Pentecost. But the significant word for us is that Simon Peter was convinced that what was happening was God's work. And it was a time for him to show that Jesus gave all that was happening its true meaning. And throughout the Book of Acts, we find that Jesus is the one who gives meaning to God's work that has reached its climax in the revelation that we know in his life, death, and resurrection. Peter begins with Jesus, with the history of God among his people. And beginning with that, he says to those who hear him, "Jesus is the point of reference whom I call to your attention in this hour."[4]

I remember so well that when I was serving my first church we had to buy some additional property. We had only the property on which the church building rested. A surveyor came one wintry day, and, because of the complications in the property lines, he spent a great deal of time establishing one point of reference. I have thought many times since then that the one point which he established that day made all the difference in the other surveying that he did. That point had to be right. And beginning with that point, he moved out. So it is that we who dream the Christian dream are reminded by our forefathers who dreamed before us that our basic point of reference is Jesus Christ. And we move out from him. The early church at its finest reminds us of what God can do in folks like you and me when we are really prepared for him to be the central point of reference in our pilgrimage.

We are reminded also that dreamers are swept along by an inner force. Now, as a matter of fact, Stewart Holbrook tells us in the recounting of the lives of these great people, that they had an almost overwhelming conviction that grew up inside them. And many of these people preferred to be defeated rather than give up their conviction. Now, in a very genuine sense, those of us who have inherited the dream of our forefathers in the Book of Acts are in a very profound sense aware that our strength is not ours, but the gift of God. At our best we know that what we are is God's gift to us. And many times, we are also aware that like many other people we are not always molded by the force within us but by the forces outside of us. We are always hoping that there will be some easy way, some outside force that will see us through, some force that we can control, some force that we can manipulate. Now, as a matter of fact, the force that lives within us is not any that is our own, that is the result of any psychologizing tonic, or the appropriation of any Stoic lecture. It is a gift beyond us. It is the gift of the God who comes to us in the present tense. But all our days we, too, have to live with the awareness that it is easy for us to hope that some outside force that we can control will really be the master of our pilgrimage.

Some of you have heard me tell a story that I want to tell again. I was in divinity school at Yale at the time. I was going out to the First Baptist Church in Essex to act as interim pastor. My wife went with me. And when we had services, my wife would sit with the superintendent of the Sunday School, his wife, and their son and daughter. The children were small, so they would sit, the little boy, my wife, the boy's mother, then his sister, then his father. And on this particular morning, my wife reminded me later, I was praying what we call the pastoral prayer (and which the laymen call the long prayer). And she said I had been especially fervent in prayer that day, praying for things in the heaven, on the earth, and under the earth. And it was the custom to keep the little fellow quiet by feeding him Life Savers. So, in the midst of this long series of petitions to the Lord, she said the little fellow reached across her lap in desperation and said to his mother, "Gimme another Life Saver!"

Well, I know what the little fellow was talking about. There are all kinds of times that we long for Life Savers that we simply take and that solve the problem. But we are called not to depend upon any force that we can conjure up, but the gift of God which is the gift of his powerful presence. And Peter, that day, reminded the church for all the years to come, that its strength is given to it. It is from beyond it. It is the gift of God who promises his power and gives it to his people.

Dreamers are a people who end with a different goal. They do not like to be different merely for themselves but for others. They want to be instruments of a new life. Surely this has been true in American history and in the history of the church. From the days of its earliest history, its mission has been the proclamation of the kingdom of God: to show forth Christ in the center of God's kingdom, to remind men and women that the marvel of our faith is not merely that we will one day go to heaven, but that one day, surely, heaven came to us. And we are called to show it forth.

Peter wrote, "You are . . . chosen . . . that you may declare the wonderful deeds of him who called you out of darkness into his marvelous light," to show forth Christ and to show forth the oneness of humanity in Christ.[5] At the very end of the Book of Acts, Paul reminds his hearers (not all of whom are happy with what he has to say) that the mission of the church, the mission of the preacher, is to declare the oneness of Jews and Gentiles in Jesus Christ. He set forth his purpose in Christ, the Scripture teaches us, to unite all things in him.

So we show forth the Christ and the oneness of humanity through him as we show forth eternity in the midst of the years. Showing forth eternity in the midst of the years— this is what the dream is all about. It is showing forth the reality of God in these present years of our lives. Again, Scripture teaches us that the hour is coming, and now is, when we enter upon the fellowship with God that is life eternal. And when we hear the word of God in the Book of Acts, and when we are reminded that it is a story of a dream come true, we pose for ourselves the question, "Do I dream the dream? Has the dream come true for me?" And we hear the words of Peter long ago, "The dream is meant for you and for your children and for all who are far away."[6]

Almighty God our Father, who has blessed our coming in, bless our going forth, that we will be strengthened to be children of light in the world thou dost love. Through Christ our Lord we pray. Amen.

19
The Grand Invitation
of Christ

Almighty God our Father, we open our hearts to thee who hast opened thy heart to us. Forgive us our sins, and renew us who have sinned against thee, and plant a right spirit within us. O Lord, we name to thee in the silence of our hearts those among us who today especially need thy loving care. Remind us that thou art the great physician who dost tend the bodies and souls of thy children. O Lord, speak thy word to us in this hour, that we may truly receive it and live it. Through Jesus Christ our Lord. Amen.

At that time Jesus answered and said, I thank thee, O Father, Lord of heaven and earth, because thou hast hid these things from the wise and prudent, and hast revealed them unto babes. Even so, Father; for so it seemed good in thy sight. All things are delivered unto me of my Father; and no man knoweth the Son, but the Father; neither knoweth any man the Father, save the Son, and he to whomsoever the Son will reveal him.

Come unto me, all ye that labour and are heavy laden, and I will give you rest. Take my yoke upon you, and learn of me; for I am meek and lowly in heart: and ye shall find rest unto your souls. For my yoke is easy, and my burden is light.

(Matthew 11:25-30, King James Version)

A chapel meditation presented on May 1, 1975.

I suppose if there is anything at the end of the term for which we have an existential feeling, it is that we are under great labor, and we are heavy-laden. I have noticed especially since March the first that my colleagues on the faculty have quickened their pace, even though for some of us that has become increasingly a heroic achievement. And in the last few days, some of us are very near to breathing threats and slaughter. And there is a sudden activity among students in the library that is a marvel to behold. I also noticed the other day that two of my most dedicated scholars (one on the left and one on the right) were more in the land of Nod than in the land of the living. It is easy for us to think of heavy labor and heavy burdens at the end of the term. But I hope that this will remind us to think of the lesson before us in very serious terms at the end of the semester also.

"Come unto me, all ye that labour and are heavy laden."[1] This invitation is directed by Jesus to devout people, to those who take their religion seriously. That means that Jesus knows that being good may be a burden and not a lift. It may be weight and not wings. Sometimes people do carry their religion; it does not carry them. So this word of Jesus is directed to those who are serious about God, but are bowed down and not lifted up by their relationship.

Now it is bad enough when life is a burden. But when our religion is a burden also, we need a voice calling to save us. More than that, this text is a word addressed to anyone for whom life itself is a drag. Life may be a burden because we have found no satisfying meaning in it, or because of interruptions, or road blocks, or dead-end streets. "All ye that labour and are heavy laden" includes all to whom there comes a longing for the meaning of life itself.

"Come." Here is the grand invitation. Here is the challenge that comes from Christ. It is an invitation to every life that possesses a sense of need. It is a call to be the companion of Jesus. It is the same call that now sounds forth what was heard first on the lake in Galilee, "Come, follow me."

"I will give you rest." That means, I think, "I will give you serenity, completion, satisfaction. I will give you the contentment that comes from genuine fulfillment. I will give you what you are now working for. I will make your spiritual dream come true. I will give true rest, the sense of the presence of God." How astounding—"Come to me, and I will give you God's presence"! How is that possible?

"Take my yoke upon you." This is the language of the fields. It is also the language of devotion. To come under the yoke is to submit to a master. But here the yoke is not submission to the law of Moses but to the Son of God. It is the submission of discipleship. So Jesus calls all who sense the need of God to come to him. Boldly he declares that allegiance to him is the clue to the meaning of life: "Yoke up your life with mine. Let me help you plow a straight furrow in the rough places of life."

I remember reading years ago in Unamuno's great book, *The Tragic Sense of Life*, that we learn what real life is when we plow hard, stony ground together beneath a common yoke. "Yoke up your life with mine. Commit yourself to me, for my yoke is easy and my burden is light." The yoke of Jesus is easy because it is the way of salvation by faith alone. The yoke of Jesus is easy because he is meek and lowly of heart, never the stern censor of failures, but the kind redeemer of sin. He who teaches faith incarnates faith because his meekness and humility mark his trust in God.

The wonderful thing about Jesus is that he makes salvation by faith alone believable. Since the days he first called out, "Come, follow me," men and women have learned that bondage to him, plowing beneath his yoke, is easy because it is perfect freedom. It is perfect freedom because through it we may grow into the maturity of the sons and daughters of God in the relationship of faith and hope and love.

Taking the yoke of Jesus means learning from Jesus. "Learn from me."[2] Only when we pass under the yoke do we learn from Jesus. Only in commitment do we find rest for our souls. There is a world of difference between looking at Jesus and looking to him. Learning from Jesus, we learn of God and find rest for our souls. But learning from Jesus does not mean the end of labor but the beginning of service. He gives us rest by giving us work, and the work he gives is carrying the cross. "Come, learn from me" is at the center of Matthew's Gospel, and "Go to the world" is at the end of it. His light in us and our light in his, that is the service that gives rest to us and to the world. Learning from Jesus means living out of Christ and living Christ out. It is that living, it is that service that brings rest to our souls.

Jesus offers us his yoke at the cross. Only there does he offer it. When that yoke is placed on our surrendered hearts, we begin to learn from him as friends learn from each other—and we need to remember that he called his disciples "friends." We learn from him by living with him and for him. We learn from him that it takes a whole lifetime to learn from him. We learn that commitment and discipleship, and discipleship and growth—life under his yoke—must be ever renewed all our days upon the earth.

Living with each other this term is drawing to its end. But our life in Christ draws nearer Christ. And in this we rejoice. Each day we live is a new summons to faith and service, an answer to the call of Jesus. Every day he calls us to come to him. And he comes to us. It is the joy of our coming to him every day that assures us that his promise comes true. We find rest for our souls. "Come. Take my yoke. Learn from me. You will find rest."

God our Father, who has blessed our coming in, bless our going forth, that we may truly do thy work in the world. Through Jesus Christ our Lord we pray. Amen.

20
The Promise of Jesus

O Lord of heaven and earth, we rejoice in thee and thy gift of salvation. We are unworthy of thy grace. And we thank thee for it. Forgive us our sins and renew our spirits by thine own. We bring thee, our Father, our hopes and disappointments, our joys and sorrows, our faith and doubts, our strength and weakness, to be blessed by thee, that we may receive the light of thy truth. Teach us to give ourselves to thee and to open our lives to thee. O thou who hast lived for us in thy Son, grant that we may never outlive our love of thee. Through Christ our Lord. Amen.

And when they were come to the place, which is called Calvary, there they crucified him, and the malefactors, one on the right hand, and the other on the left. Then said Jesus, Father, forgive them; for they know not what they do. And they parted his raiment, and cast lots. And the people stood beholding. And the rulers also with them derided him, saying, He saved others; let him save himself, if he be Christ, the chosen of God. And the soldiers also mocked him, coming to him, and offering him vinegar, And saying, If thou be the King of the Jews, save thyself. And a superscription also was written over him in letters of Greek, and Latin, and Hebrew, THIS IS THE KING OF THE JEWS. And one of the

A chapel meditation presented on April 7, 1976.

malefactors which were hanged railed on him, saying, If thou be Christ, save thyself and us. But the
other answering rebuked him, saying, Dost not thou
fear God, seeing thou art in the same condemnation?
And we indeed justly; for we receive the due reward
of our deeds: but this man hath done nothing amiss.
And he said unto Jesus, Lord, remember me when
thou comest into thy kingdom. And Jesus said unto
him, Verily I say unto thee, To-day shalt thou be with
me in paradise.

(Luke 23:33-43, King James Version)

No words are dearer to us than the words of Jesus when
he was dying. Some of the most solemn sermons and the
most poignant music of the church set forth these words as
a precious treasure. For a long time, and for a special
reason, I have liked the words addressed to the penitent
criminal who was hanging beside Jesus, "Today thou shalt
be with me in paradise."[1]

Careful study of the last words of Jesus indicates that they
are the confession of faith. Here is not so much history as
confession. In these words are the revelation of the meaning of Jesus to the faithful. The words spoken from the cross
tell the story of the cross and the crucified. They are the
story of our faith in the Son of God. In the story of Jesus and
the two criminals we find the gospel we proclaim as life.
Jesus is surrounded by the mighty of the sword and the
soul, and by the taunts of the cynical and the disbelieving.

From the midst of them, there emerges a most unlikely
hero of the spirit. We do not know his name. We only know
his calling. He was a criminal. It is reasonable to believe
that he was being crucified because he was a Zealot, who
had taken his sword in hand against Rome. He was learning
that those who take the sword perish by the sword. And, in

dying, he met the man in the middle, Christ on his cross.

As we read the story, our minds and our hearts are drawn to Jesus and that criminal. And from those two crosses is spoken the word of life. As surely as we live, just as surely do we die. So let us hold dear this word, "Today thou shalt be with me in paradise."

Three times, according to Luke's Gospel, those who are party to the death of Jesus laugh at him. The people stood looking on; their rulers jeered at him. The soldiers joined the mockery. And one criminal on a cross taunted him. "Save yourself and come down," they said. And Luke records the sad words, "His friends had all been standing at a distance; the women who had accompanied him from Galilee stood with them and watched it all."[2] Jesus was alone with his enemies and a criminal and the gospel. Three times the enemies of Jesus scorned him, and three times Jesus was silent. How often faith and hope and love are silent because they are strong.

Suddenly a criminal was on the center of the stage and spoke a good word for Jesus. Jesus was all alone except for a criminal who cried out on that hill of injustice, "This man has done nothing wrong."[3] That is one thing I have always liked about this unlikely hero—he spoke up for Jesus. He had confidence in Jesus. Rulers and priests condemned him, and only a criminal told the truth. How terrible, but true, that those who ought to know so much understand so little and that those who ought to know so little understand so much. That was the way it always was and has been with Jesus. Those on the inside are on the outside and those on the outside are on the inside. It took a sinner to know Jesus. And it still does, too. "I know thee who thou art."[4] That is what the needy have confessed in faith always. And we have known him because he has known us.

In the second place, the criminal expressed faith in

Jesus. He believed that Jesus was the difference between life and death: "Lord, remember me when thou comest into thy kingdom." That is a confession of faith. Nobody else up to that time had expressed faith in the man in the middle, dying on a cross. In the presence of the crucified, the criminal learned who Jesus is and who he is. Powerful representatives of church and state scorned Jesus, but a criminal saw him.

That was the way it was when he was born. The lowly were the first at his cradle; the lowly were the first at his cross—"Lord, remember me when thou comest into thy kingdom." Outcasts greeted him as he entered the world. And outcasts greeted him as he entered the world to come. This story of two crosses is the story of a sinner and a Savior. That story is our story. In the presence of Jesus on his cross we have learned who he is and we have learned who we are. We know we are sinners and he is our Savior. This story is our story. Let us find in the heart of the thief our own, "Lord, remember me."

In the third place, we learn that the criminal had faith in Jesus because he confessed his need. Oh, how often Jesus rejoiced as he walked about Galilee and heard people say to him, "Help me! Help me!" The doorway to the kingdom of God is a cry for help, "Lord, have mercy upon me!" To such belongs the kingdom of God. I do not know how long that criminal had lived with lawlessness. But once he met the man in the middle, he wanted to live with him in his kingdom. The power of the sword gave way to the power of the cross. And the power of rebellion gave way to the power of faith.

And then the light turned on Jesus as he said, "Today thou shalt be with me in paradise." Where faith is, Jesus is. Jesus died the way he lived, thinking of others. Bound to God in faith, he bound himself to sinners in love. And he made a promise—"Today you will share with me in paradise."

It is not given to faith to fling open the gates of paradise and see the mysteries of God. But it is given to faith to be with Jesus. We have the promise, because Jesus made it a long time ago to another sinner, "Today you will share with me in paradise." Jesus promises us a future when we have no future. When we have no present, he gives us a present. "Today. Today. With me." The dying man only asked for tomorrow, and the dying Lord gave him today. And more than that, Jesus gave himself—"Today you will be with me." It is good to be promised tomorrow; it is better to be promised today; it is best of all to be promised Jesus.

Jesus did not come down from the cross because he wanted to come to us and take us to him. Let us give thanks to God for the criminal who was hanging at Jesus' side. From him we learn that if we give our hearts to Christ, he gives us his peace.

On April 17, 1957, at five o'clock in the morning, trusted physicians in Richmond, Virginia, told my wife and me that our four-year old son was dead. He had lost an eight-month fight with cancer. At eight o'clock that morning, I looked out the front door and saw Dr. Ted Adams walking to the house. He was God's gift of an angel to us. On Good Friday we laid our Bryan in the ground. He used to pray with his eyes open, so he could see, he said, what to thank God for. And he said once in his sickness, "God is the best man in the whole world."

With the dogwood trees a fairyland and the azaleas bright with bloom, we walked across the rich green grass of spring and laid him in the ground. God's great gift to me that day was Christ's word to a penitent criminal, "Today thou shalt be with me in paradise." Surely a God of grace who opens the gates of paradise to a long life that has been evil will open them to a short life that has been good. On Easter Sunday I preached the gospel of the resurrection. Christ has opened paradise! Hallelujah!

Good Friday is near us; and Easter is not so far away. Perhaps not so long ago you made that long day's journey to the grave with one you love. As surely as you live, you will. Let us gather around that cross of a penitent criminal, and let us hear the good news of the gospel, "Today thou shalt be with me in paradise."

> May I fight befriended,
> And see in my last strife
> To me thine arms extended
> Upon the cross of life.[5]

O Lord, who has blessed our coming in, bless our going forth, that we may journey with thee. Through Christ our Lord. Amen.

Notes

Introduction

1. Charles K. Barrett, *Biblical Problems and Biblical Preaching* (Philadelphia: Fortress Press, 1964), p. 48.

Chapter 1: When God's Love Floods the Heart

1. 1 Peter 2:21-24.
2. John 12:27-28a.
3. Cited in William Barclay, *A New Testament Wordbook* (London: SCM Press, 1955), p. 61.
4. 1 Thessalonians 5:16-18.
5. Jeremiah 12:5.
6. Hebrews 5:8-9 (author's italics).
7. Psalm 27:1, Goodspeed's translation.
8. See Romans 5:4b.
9. Romans 5:8.
10. Source unknown. It is probably from Paul Tillich or Sören Kierkegaard.
11. 1 Peter 1:3, Goodspeed's translation.
12. Traditional hymn from Rippon's *Selection of Hymns from the Best Authors*, 1787.
13. Romans 5:5, Goodspeed's translation.
14. William Williams, "Guide Me, O Thou Great Jehovah," *Baptist Hymnal* (Nashville: Convention Press, 1956), p. 56.
15. John 16:33b.
16. Romans 8:28.
17. Daniel 3:25, Moffatt's translation.
18. Romans 8:38-39.
19. Romans 5:5, Goodspeed's translation.

Chapter 2: A Little Child Shall Lead Them

1. Isaiah 11:6c, King James Version.

2. Sören Kierkegaard, *The Gospel of Suffering and the Lilies of the Field*, trans. David F. Swenson and Lillian Marvin Swenson (Minneapolis: Augsburg Publishing House, 1948), p. 64.

3. Ibid., p. 61.

4. Samuel Rutherford, *Trial and Triumph of Faith* (Wheeling, Va.: W. Wilson, 1840), p. 73.

5. Isaiah 43:1c-2b, King James Version.

6. 2 Corinthians 12:9a, King James Version.

7. Authorship uncertain, "O Sacred Head, Now Wounded," *Baptist Hymnal* (Nashville: Convention Press, 1956), p. 91.

8. John 14:1a, King James Version; John 14:18a (author's translation).

9. Baron Friedrich von Hügel, *Selected Letters, 1896-1924*, ed. Bernard Holland (London: J. M. Dent and Sons, 1928), p. 228.

10. John Bunyan, *The Pilgrim's Progress*, ed. Charles W. Eliot, in *The Harvard Classics*, vol. 15 (New York: P. F. Collier and Son, 1909), p. 161.

11. Malcolm James McLeod, *Letters to Edward* (New York: Fleming H. Revell and Company, 1913), p. 185.

12. Sören Kierkegaard, *The Gospel of Suffering*, p. 32.

13. Hebrews 11:13c, King James Version.

14. 2 Corinthians 4:17-18, American Standard Version © 1901, Thomas Nelson & Sons.

15. John Bunyan, *The Pilgrim's Progress*, p. 68.

16. Sören Kierkegaard, *The Gospel of Suffering*, p. 20.

17. Max Muller, in John Baillie, *A Diary of Readings* (London: Oxford University Press, 1955), p. 124.

18. John Bunyan, *The Pilgrim's Progress*, p. 320.

19. Psalm 103:1, King James Version.

Chapter 3: Lift Up Your Hearts!

1. Luke 12:32; Matthew 26:53.

2. Authorship uncertain, "O Sacred Head, Now Wounded," *Baptist Hymnal* (Nashville: Convention Press, 1956), p. 91.

3. Luke 24:21, Moffatt's translation.

4. John Donne, "Elegie: Death," *The Complete Poetry and Selected Prose of John Donne and The Complete Poetry of William Blake*, with an Introduction by Robert Silliman Hillyer (New York: Random House, 1941), p. 209.

5. Edwin Markham, "Who Was Christus?" *Poems of Edwin Mark-*

ham, ed. Charles L. Wallis (New York: Harper and Brothers, 1950), p. 100.

6. John 21:3, King James Version.

7. John 16:32*b*.

8. John 16:33*b*.

9. Roland Bainton, *Here I Stand: A Life of Martin Luther* (New York: Abingdon-Cokesbury Press, 1950), p. 370.

10. Athanasius, *The Incarnation of the Word of God, Being the Treatise of St. Athanasius,* trans. by a religious of C. S. M. V., S. th (New York: The Macmillan Company, 1946), p. 54.

11. Karl Barth, *Dogmatics in Outline,* trans. G. T. Thomson (London: SCM Press, 1955), p. 123.

12. Henry M. Butler, "Lift Up Your Hearts," *The Student Hymnary,* ed. Edward Dwight Eaton (New York: A. S. Barnes and Company, 1939), p. 178.

Chapter 4: How Lovely Is Thy Dwelling Place

1. Psalm 87:2-3, King James Version.

2. Walter Rauschenbusch, "The Postern Gate," in Dores R. Sharpe, *Walter Rauschenbusch* (New York: The Macmillan Company, 1942), pp. 451-52.

3. Cecil F. Alexander, "There Is a Green Hill Far Away," *Baptist Hymnal* (Nashville: Convention Press, 1956), p. 98.

4. Dietrich Bonhoeffer, *Life Together,* trans. John W. Doberstein (New York: Harper and Row, 1954), p. 20.

5. Artur Weiser, *The Psalms: A Commentary,* trans. Herbert Hartwell (London: SCM Press, 1962), p. 568.

6. Paraphrase of Philippians 4:13.

7. Paraphrase of Psalm 84:6.

8. Harold A. Bosley, *Sermons on the Psalms* (New York: Harper and Row, 1956), p. 76.

Chapter 5: Remember Jesus Christ

1. Paraphrase of Deuteronomy 26:8.

2. Roland Bainton, *Here I Stand: A Life of Martin Luther* (New York: Abingdon-Cokesbury Press, 1950), p. 370.

3. Elizabeth Barrett Browning, "Sonnets From the Portuguese," Sonnet VII. See *The Victorian Age: Prose, Poetry, and Drama,* ed. John W. Bowyer and John L. Brooks, 2nd ed. (New York: Appleton-Century-Crofts, 1954), p. 325. Reprinted by permission of Prentice-Hall, Inc., Englewood Cliffs, N.J.

4. Charles Wesley, "Christ the Lord Is Risen Today," *Baptist Hymnal* (Nashville: Convention Press, 1975), p. 114.

5. 2 Corinthians 5:20.

Chapter 6: There Is No Prison for the Word of God

1. The Moffatt translation uniquely renders this passage, "But there is no prison for the word of God." This brilliant rendering is reiterated throughout this sermon. As noted in the introduction, unless otherwise indicated, all other Scripture quotations are from the Revised Standard Version.

2. Ephesians 6:12.

3. Dietrich Bonhoeffer, *Letters and Papers from Prison,* ed. Eberhard Bethge (London: SCM Press, 1953), p. 162.

4. Luke 4:18, paraphrase.

5. Mark 16:7.

6. Psalm 103:1.

Chapter 7: The Knowledge of God

1. John Calvin, *Institutes of the Christian Religion,* trans. Henry Beveridge (London: James Clarke and Co., 1953), pp. 37,38.

2. Jeremiah 9:23-24.

3. Galatians 4:9.

4. Matthew 11:27*b*.

5. John 8:31-32.

Chapter 8: I Am Here to Serve the Lord

1. A paraphrased form of the scriptural conversation between Mary and the angel is used frequently in this meditation.

2. Christina G. Rossetti, "A Christmas Carol." See *Worship Resources for the Christian Year,* ed. Charles L. Wallis (New York: Harper and Row, 1954), p. 24.

Chapter 9: Loving God with Heart, Soul, and Mind

1. Mark 12:30-31.

2. H. Richard Niebuhr, *The Purpose of the Church and Its Ministry* (New York: Harper and Row, 1956), pp. 35-36.

3. Ibid., p. 38.

4. Paraphrase.

5. Paraphrase.

6. Dante Alighieri, *The Divine Comedy,* 33. 82-87, trans. Jefferson B. Fletcher (New York: Columbia University Press, 1951), p. 469. Used by permission.

Chapter 10: The Fire on the Altar

1. Leviticus 6:12. All quotations from Scripture in this sermon are from *The New English Bible*.

2. 2 Timothy 1:6.

3. Ancient Irish verse; trans. Mary Byrne and versified by Eleanor Hull, "Be Thou My Vision," *The Poem Book of the Gael*, ed. Eleanor Hull; by permission of the Editor's Literary Estate and Chatto & Windus Ltd.

4. Thomas Moore, "Come, Ye Disconsolate," *Baptist Hymnal* (Nashville: Convention Press, 1975), p. 211.

5. Eugene O'Neill, *Long Day's Journey into Night* (New Haven: Yale University Press, 1955), p. 78. Used by permission.

6. Edwin Hatch, "Breathe on Me, Breath of God," *Baptist Hymnal* (Nashville: Convention Press, 1975), p. 317.

7. Charles Wesley, "O Thou Who Camest from Above," *The Methodist Hymnal*, ed. Carlton R. Young (Nashville: The Methodist Publishing House, 1966), p. 172.

Chapter 11: The Hidden and Revealed God

1. Karl Barth, *Church Dogmatics* II, 1, ed. G. W. Bromiley and T. F. Torrance, trans. T. H. L. Parker (Edinburgh: T. and T. Clark, 1957), p. 182.

2. Isaiah 45:15, King James Version.

3. 1 Corinthians 2:9, *Today's English Version*.

4. Matthew 11:25.

5. 1 John 3:2.

Chapter 12: Free in Christ

1. Galatians 5:1, *Today's English Version*.

2. Charles Wesley, "O for a Thousand Tongues to Sing," *Baptist Hymnal* (Nashville: Convention Press, 1975), p. 69.

3. George Matheson, "Make Me A Captive, Lord," *The Baptist Hymn Book* (London: Psalms and Hymns Trust, 1974), p. 478.

Chapter 13: Treasure in Earthen Vessels

1. Paraphrase.

2. Philippians 3:10-11.

Chapter 14: Heralds of Good Tidings

1. The King James Version of this verse is used throughout this meditation.

2. Halford Luccock, *Marching Off the Map* (New York: Harper and Brothers, 1952), p. 81.

3. Isaiah 52:7, King James Version.

4. Paraphrase.

5. Luke 2:10, King James Version.

6. Isaiah 40:9.

Chapter 15: A Presence That Disturbs Me

1. William Wordsworth, "Lines Composed a Few Miles Above Tintern Abbey," *Wordsworth: Poetry and Prose,* ed. W. M. Merchant (Cambridge: Harvard University Press, 1967), p. 154.

2. Luke 24:32.

3. Revelation 3:20.

4. Augustine, *The Confessions of St. Augustine,* trans. Rex Warner (New York: The New American Library, 1963), pp. 184-85.

5. Karl Barth, *Deliverance to the Captives,* trans. Marguerite Wieser (New York: Harper and Row, 1961), pp. 46-47.

Chapter 17: "Sir, We Want to See Jesus"

1. Harry W. Farrington, "I Know Not How that Bethlehem's Babe," *Baptist Hymnal* (Nashville: Convention Press, 1956), p. 276.

2. Dietrich Bonhoeffer, *The Cost of Discipleship,* rev. ed., trans. R. H. Fuller and revised by Irmgard Booth (New York: The Macmillan Company, 1959), p. 54.

3. See ibid., pp. 35-47.

Chapter 18: Dreamers of the Dream

1. See Stewart H. Holbrook, *Dreamers of the American Dream* (Garden City: Doubleday, 1957).

2. Paraphrase of Acts 2:39.

3. Albert E. Day, *An Autobiography of Prayer* (New York: Harper and Brothers, 1952), pp. 26-27.

4. Paraphrase.

5. 1 Peter 2:9, paraphrase; quoted portion from the Revised Standard Version.

6. Paraphrase.

Chapter 19: The Grand Invitation of Christ

1. The text given with this meditation is from the King James Version. Direct quotations of the text (not paraphrased quotations) are from that version.

2. Most modern translations render Jesus' words, "learn from me." Professor Brown has drawn on the insight of these recent versions.

Chapter 20: The Promise of Jesus

1. Throughout this meditation, Professor Brown's phrasing of the promise to the criminal obviously relies on the King James Version but is modernized a bit.   -

2. Luke 23:49, *The New English Bible*.

3. Luke 23:41, *The New English Bible*.

4. Mark 1:24, King James Version.

5. Source unknown.